New Selected Poems

Also by Edwin Morgan from Carcanet:

Collected Poems
Collected Translations
Virtual and Other Realities

translations:

Jean Racine, *Phaedra*
Edmond Rostand, *Cyrano de Bergerac*

Edwin Morgan

New Selected Poems

CARCANET

Acknowledgements

Planet Wave, a sequence of ten poems commissioned by the Cheltenham Jazz Festival, and set to music by Tommy Smith, was first performed in the Cheltenham Town Hall on 4 April 1997, and is reprinted here from *PN Review*.

Published in Great Britain in 2000 by
Carcanet Press Limited
4th Floor, Conavon Court
12-16 Blackfriars Street
Manchester M3 5BQ

A CIP catalogue record for this book
is available from the British Library.

ISBN 1 85754 459 5

The publisher acknowledges financial
assistance from the Arts Council of England.

Set in 10pt Palatino by Bryan Williamson, Frome

Printed and bound in England by SRP Ltd, Exeter.

Contents

Stanzas of the Jeopardy

It may be at midday, limousines in cities, the groaning
Derrick and hissing hawser alive at dockyards,
Liners crawling with heat-baked decks, their élite
Drinking languid above the hounded turbines,
Doorways and crossroads thronged with a hundred rendezvous,
Planes low over spire and cupola with screaming
Jet-streams or soaring inaudible in disembodied calm,
Plough-teams on headlands in the sweat of noon, the warm
Earth up-ruffled swarming for crow and gull,
Boys whistling and calling at play in the sea-caves,
Cables humming, telephonists sighing, sirens
Wailing twelve from workshop and factory, tar
Bubbling in the skin of the street, shopfronts shimmering,
In Times Square, Leicester Square, Red Square – that the roar, the
    labour,
The onset and the heat, the engine and the flurry and the errand,
The plane and the phone and the plough and the farm, the farmer
And the stoker and the airman and the docker and the shopper
    and the boy
Shall all be called to a halt:
In the middle of the day, and in the twinkling of an eye.

It could be at midnight, braziers smouldering on wharves,
Watchmen dozing by the tar-boiler's hulk, warehouses
Planted gloomily in bloodless night-idleness,
Desolate siding and shed and circuit littered
With the truck and trash marooned by ebbing daytime,
Astronomers at their mirrors in zodiacal quiet, dancers
Swept through the rosy fantasy of muted waltzes,
Children speaking to the wind and stars in dream,
Great lakes of darkness mountain-locked and moonless
Breaking to the meagre splash of angler's oar,
Badger and hedgehog rooting among the beech-mast, gardens
Swirling with scents disessenced by the dawn,
Lovers lying in the dunes of summer, swimmers
Flashing like sudden fire in the bay – that the play,
The sleep and the pleasure, the tryst, the glow, the tranquillity,
The water and the silence, the fragrance, the vigil and the kiss,
The fishermen and the slumberers and the whisperers and the
    creatures of the wood

Shall craze to an intolerable blast
And hear at midnight the very end of the world.

'Shall the trumpet sound before the suns have cooled?
Shall there not be portents of blood, sea-beds laid bare,
Concrete and girder like matchwood in earthquake and whirlwind?
Shall we not see the angels, or the creeping icecap, or the moon
Falling, or the wandering star, feel veins boiling
Or fingers freezing or the wind thickening with wings?'
The earth may spin beyond apocalypse;
Long before entropy the worlds may stop.
The heart praises its own intentions, while the moment,
The neighbour, the need, the face of love and the tears
Have passed unseized, as some day they will pass
Beyond all action, beyond despair and redemption,
When matter has uttered its last sound, when the eye
That roved around the universe goes blind, when lips
To lips are numb, when space is rolled away
And time is torn from its rings, and the door of life
Flies open on unimaginable things –
At noon, at midnight, or at no time,
As you receive these verses, O Corinthians.

Verses for a Christmas Card

This endyir starnacht blach and klar
As I on Cathkin-fells held fahr
A snaepuss fussball showerdown
With nezhny smirl and whirlcome rown
Upon my pollbare underlift,
And smazzled all my gays with srift:
Faroer fieldswhide frosbloom strayfling,
Froral brookrims hoartrack glassling,
Allairbelue beauheaven ablove
Avlanchbloomfondshowed brrumalljove.

O angellighthoused harbourmoon,
Glazegulfgalaxeval governoon,
Jovegal allcapellar jupiterror
And you brighdsun of venusacre,
Respour this leidyear Phoenixmas
With starphire and restorying dazz
Bejeweleavening cinderill
To liftlike pace and goodquadrille.
All men reguard, from grace our fere,
And sun on us to kind and chere.

Message Clear

```
    am              i
                        if
i am                    he
      he r         o
      h     ur   t
      the re           and
      he      re      and
      he re
  a               n   d
      the r               e
i am     r                ife
                i  n
            s       ion and
i                       d     i e
   am   e res    ect
   am   e res    ection
                      o           f
      the                     life
                      o           f
    m   e             n
            sur e
      the               d     i e
i          s
            s    e t     and
i am the   sur          d
   a   t    res    t
                      o           life
i am  he r                    e
i a          ct
i       r  u      n
i  m   e e     t
i          t              i e
i       s   t    and
i am th           o        th
i am     r          a
i am the   su        n
i am the   s        on
i am the  e    rect on      e if
i am     re        n    t
i am       s         a       fe
```

12

```
i am    s     e     n      t
i    he e                 d
i     t e  s       t
i      re             a d
 a   th re             a d
 a      s     t on        e
 a   t   re             a d
 a   th r        on         e
i          resurrect
                     a        life
i am                i n         life
i am      resurrection
i am the resurrection and
i am
i am the resurrection and the life
```


Strawberry Fields Forever

my blackie

                                                    smirr

   losing

                  foxpaw

       patter

                     your hazel

          whistle

                 dewdrop

    kneedeep

            unreal

                          the fields we

13

Archives

```
generation upon
generation upon
generation upon
generation upon
generation upon
generation upon
generation upon
generation upon
generation upon
generation upon
generation upon
generation upon
generation upon
generation upon
generation upon
generation upon
generation upon
generation upon
generation upon
g neration upon
g neration up  n
g nerat on up  n
g nerat  n up  n
g nerat  n  p  n
g  erat  n  p  n
g  era   n  p  n
g  era   n     n
g  er    n     n
g   r    n     n
g        n     n
g        n
g
```

14

Starryveldt

starryveldt
  slave
southvenus
  serve
SHARPEVILLE
  shove
shriekvolley
  swerve
shootvillage
  save
spoorvengeance
  stave
spadevoice
  starve
strikevault
  strive
subvert
  starve
smashverwoerd
  strive
scattervoortrekker
  starve
spadevow
  strive
sunvast
  starve
survive
  strive
SO: VAEVICTIS

Siesta of a Hungarian Snake

s   sz   sz   SZ   sz   SZ   sz   ZS   zs   ZS   zs   zs   z

```
j o l l y m e r r y
h o l l y b e r r y
j o l l y b e r r y
m e r r y h o l l y
h a p p y j o l l y
j o l l y j e l l y
j e l l y b e l l y
b e l l y m e r r y
h o l l y h e p p y
j o l l y M o l l y
m a r r y J e r r y
m e r r y H a r r y
h o p p y B a r r y
h e p p y J a r r y
b o p p y h e p p y
b e r r y j o r r y
j o r r y j o l l y
m o p p y j e l l y
M o l l y m e r r y
J e r r y j o l l y
b e l l y b o p p y
j o r r y h o p p y
h o l l y m o p p y
B a r r y m e r r y
J a r r y h a p p y
h a p p y b o p p y
b o p p y j o l l y
j o l l y m e r r y
m e r r y m e r r y
m e r r y m e r r y
m e r r y C h r i s
a m m e r r y a s a
C h r i s m e r r y
a s M E R R Y C H R
Y S A N T H E M U M
```

Opening the Cage

14 variations on 14 words

I have nothing to say and I am saying it and that is poetry.
John Cage

I have to say poetry and is that nothing and am I saying it
I am and I have poetry to say and is that nothing saying it
I am nothing and I have poetry to say and that is saying it
I that am saying poetry have nothing and it is I and to say
And I say that I am to have poetry and saying it is nothing
I am poetry and nothing and saying it is to say that I have
To have nothing is poetry and I am saying that and I say it
Poetry is saying I have nothing and I am to say that and it
Saying nothing I am poetry and I have to say that and it is
It is and I am and I have poetry saying say that to nothing
It is saying poetry to nothing and I say I have and am that
Poetry is saying I have it and I am nothing and to say that
And that nothing is poetry I am saying and I have to say it
Saying poetry is nothing and to that I say I am and have it

Chinese Cat

```
p m r k g n i a o u
p m r k g n i a o
p m r k n i a o
p m r n i a o
p m r i a o
p m i a o
m i a o
m a o
```

Clydesdale

go
   fetlocksnow
         go
           gullfurrow
                go
go
   brassglow
        go
           sweatflow
               go
go
   plodknow
        go
          clodshow
              go
go
   leatherbelow
        go
          potatothrow
                 go
go
   growfellow
        go
          crowfollow
              go
go
   Balerno
        go
          Palermo
            whoa

Centaur

i am, horse
unhorse, me
i am, horse
unhorse, me
i am, horse
unhorse, me
i am, horse
unhorse, me
i am, horse
unhorse, me
i am, horse
unhorse, me
i am, horse
unhorse, me
i am horse:
unhorse me!

The Old Man and the Sea

And a white mist rolled out of the Pacific
and crept over the sand, stirring nothing –
cold, cold as nothing is cold
on those living highways, moved in
over the early morning trucks,
chilling the drivers in their cabins
(one stops for a paper cup
of coffee, stares out through the steam
at the mist, his hands on the warm cup
imagine the coldness, he throws out the cup
and swears as the fog rolls in, drives on
frowning to feel its touch on his face) –
and seagulls came to shriek at cockcrow
swooping through the wakening farms,
and the smoke struggled from the lumber camps
up into the smoke from the sea,
hovered in the sunless morning
as a lumberman whistled at the pump,
and sea-mist took the flash from the axe.
And above the still lakes of Oregon
and the Blue Mountains into Idaho
eastward, white wings brushing the forests,
a white finger probing the canyon
by Wood River, delicate, persistent, at last
finding by the half-light, in a house of stone,
a white-bearded man like an old sea-captain
cleaning a gun. – Keep back the sea,
keep back the sea! No reassurance
in that daybreak with no sun,
his blood thin, flesh patched and scarred,
eyes grown weary of hunting
and the great game all uncaught.
It was too late to fight the sea.
The raised barrel hardly gleamed
in that American valley, the shot
insulted the morning, crude and quick
with the end of a great writer's life –
fumbling nothing, but leaving questions
that echo beyond Spain and Africa.
Questions, not answers, chill the heart here,

a chained dog whining in the straw,
the gunsmoke marrying the sea-mist,
and silence of the inhuman valleys.

The Death of Marilyn Monroe

What innocence? Whose guilt? What eyes? Whose breast?
Crumpled orphan, nembutal bed,
white hearse, Los Angeles,
DiMaggio! Los Angeles! Miller! Los Angeles! America!
That Death should seem the only protector –
That all arms should have faded, and the great cameras and lights
     become an inquisition and a torment –
That the many acquaintances, the autograph-hunters, the
     inflexible directors, the drive-in admirers should become
     a blur of incomprehension and pain –
That lonely Uncertainty should limp up, grinning, with
     bewildering barbiturates, and watch her undress and lie
     down and in her anguish
call for him! call for him to strengthen her with what could
     only dissolve her! A method
of dying, we are shaken, we see it. Strasberg!
Los Angeles! Olivier! Los Angeles! Others die
and yet by this death we are a little shaken, we feel it,
America.
Let no one say communication is a cantword.
They had to lift her hand from the bedside telephone.
But what she had not been able to say
perhaps she had said. 'All I had was my life.
I have no regrets, because if I made
any mistakes, I was responsible.
There is now – and there is the future.
What has happened is behind. So
it follows you around? So what?' – This
to a friend, ten days before.
And so she was responsible.
And if she was not responsible, not wholly responsible, Los
     Angeles? Los Angeles? Will it follow you around? Will the slow
     white hearse of the child of America follow you around?

The White Rhinoceros
'Rare over most of its former range'
Webster's Third New International Dictionary

The white rhinoceros was eating phosphorus!
I came up and I shouted Oh no! No! No! –
you'll be extinct in two years! But he shook his ears
and went on snorting, knee-deep in pawpaws,
trundling his hunger, shrugged off the tick-birds,
rolled up his sleeves, kicked over an anthill,
crunched, munched, wonderful windfall,
empty dish. And gored that old beat-up tin tray
for more, it stuck on his horn,
looked up with weird crown on his horn
like a bear with a beehive, began to glow –
as leerie lair bear glows honeybrown –
but he glowed
               white and
                     bright and
the safety-catches started to click in the thickets
for more. Run, holy hide – take up your armour –
Run – white horn, tin clown, crown of rain-woods,
venerable shiner! Run, run, run!

And thunders glowing like a phantom
through the bush, beating the guns
this time, but will he always
when his only camouflage
is a world of white?

Save the vulnerable shiners.
Watch the phosphorus trappers.
Smash the poisonous dish.

Aberdeen Train

Rubbing a glistening circle
on the steamed-up window I framed
a pheasant in a field of mist.
The sun was a great red thing somewhere low,
struggling with the milky scene. In the furrows
a piece of glass winked into life,
hypnotized the silly dandy; we
hooted past him with his head cocked,
contemplating a bottle-end.
And this was the last of October,
a Chinese moment in the Mearns.

Canedolia

An Off-Concrete Scotch Fantasia

oa! hoy! awe! ba! mey!

who saw?
rhu saw rum. garve saw smoo. nigg saw tain. lairg saw lagg.
rigg saw eigg. largs saw haggs. tongue saw luss. mull saw yell.
stoer saw strone. drem saw muck. gask saw noss. unst saw cults.
echt saw banff. weem saw wick. trool saw twatt.

how far?
from largo to lunga from joppa to skibo from ratho to shona from
ulva to minto from tinto to tolsta from soutra to marsco from
braco to barra from alva to stobo from fogo to fada from gigha to
gogo from kelso to stroma from hirta to spango.

what is it like there?
och it's freuchie, it's faifley, it's wamphray, it's frandy, it's
sliddery.

what do you do?
we foindle and fungle, we bonkle and meigle and maxpoffle. we scotstarvit, armit, wormit, and even whifflet. we play at crossstobs, leuchars, gorbals, and finfan. we scavaig, and there's aye a bit of tilquhilly. if it's wet, treshnish and mishnish.

what is the best of the country?
blinkbonny! airgold! thundergay!

and the worst?
scrishven, shiskine, scrabster, and snizort.

listen! what's that?
catacol and wauchope, never heed them.

tell us about last night
well, we had a wee ferintosh and we lay on the quiraing. it was pure strontian!

but who was there?
petermoidart and craigenkenneth and cambusputtock and ecclemuchty and corriehulish and balladolly and altnacanny and clauchanvrechan and stronachlochan and auchenlachar and tighnacrankie and tilliebruaich and killieharra and invervannach and achnatudlem and machrishellach and inchtamurchan and auchterfechan and kinlochculter and ardnawhallie and invershuggle.

and what was the toast?
schiehallion! schiehallion! schiehallion!

To Joan Eardley

Pale yellow letters
humbly straggling across
the once brilliant red
of a broken shop-face
CONFECTIO
and a blur of children
at their games, passing,
gazing as they pass
at the blur of sweets
in the dingy, cosy
Rottenrow window –
an Eardley on my wall.
Such rags and streaks
that master us! –
that fix what the pick
and bulldozer have crumbled
to a dingier dust,
the living blur
fiercely guarding
energy that has vanished,
cries filling still
the unechoing close!
I wandered by the rubble
and the houses left standing
kept a chill, dying life
in their islands of stone.
No window opened
as the coal cart rolled
and the coalman's call
fell coldly to the ground.
But the shrill children
jump on my wall.

Good Friday

Three o'clock. The bus lurches
round into the sun. 'D's this go –'
he flops beside me – 'right along Bath Street?
– Oh tha's, tha's all right, see I've
got to get some Easter eggs for the kiddies.
I've had a wee drink, ye understand –
ye'll maybe think it's a – funny day
to be celebrating – well, no, but ye see
I wasny working, and I like to celebrate
when I'm no working – I don't say it's right
I'm no saying it's right, ye understand – ye understand?
But anyway tha's the way I look at it –
I'm no boring you, eh? – ye see today,
take today, I don't know what today's in aid of,
whether Christ was – crucified or was he –
rose fae the dead like, see what I mean?
You're an educatit man, you can tell me –
– Aye, well. There ye are. It's been seen
time and again, the working man
has nae education, he jist canny – jist
hasny got it, know what I mean,
he's jist bliddy ignorant – Christ aye,
bliddy ignorant. Well –' The bus brakes violently,
he lunges for the stair, swings down – off,
into the sun for his Easter eggs,
on very
      nearly
          steady
             legs.

The Starlings in George Square

I

Sundown on the high stonefields!
The darkening roofscape stirs –
thick – alive with starlings
gathered singing in the square –
like a shower of arrows they cross
the flash of a western window,
they bead the wires with jet,
they nestle preening by the lamps
and shine, sidling by the lamps
and sing, shining, they stir
the homeward hurrying crowds.
A man looks up and points
smiling to his son beside him
wide-eyed at the clamour on those cliffs –
it sinks, shrills out in waves,
levels to a happy murmur,
scatters in swooping arcs,
a stab of confused sweetness
that pierces the boy like a story,
a story more than a song.
He will never forget that evening,
the silhouette of the roofs,
the starlings by the lamps.

II

The City Chambers are hopping mad.
Councillors with rubber plugs in their ears!
Secretaries closing windows!
Window-cleaners want protection and danger money.
The Lord Provost can't hear herself think, man.
What's that?
Lord Provost, can't hear herself think.

At the General Post Office
the clerks write Three Pounds Starling in the savings-books.
Each telephone-booth is like an aviary.
I tried to send a parcel to County Kerry but –

The cables to Cairo got fankled, sir.
What's that?
I said the cables to Cairo got fankled.

And as for the City Information Bureau –
I'm sorry I can't quite chirrup did you twit –
No I wanted to twee but perhaps you can't cheep –
Would you try once again, that's better, I – sweet –
When's the last boat to Milngavie? Tweet?
What's that?
I said when's the last boat to Milngavie?

III

There is nothing for it now but scaffolding:
clamp it together, send for the bird-men,
Scarecrow Strip for the window-ledge landings,
Cameron's Repellent on the overhead wires.
Armour our pediments against eavesdroppers.
This is a human outpost. Save our statues.
Send back the jungle. And think of the joke:
as it says in the papers, It is very comical
to watch them alight on the plastic rollers
and take a tumble. So it doesn't kill them?
All right, so who's complaining? This isn't Peking
where they shoot the sparrows for hygiene and cash.
So we're all humanitarians, locked in our cliff-dwellings
encased in our repellent, guano-free and guilt-free.
The Lord Provost sings in her marble hacienda.
The Postmaster-General licks an audible stamp.
Sir Walter is vexed that his column's deserted.
I wonder if we really deserve starlings?
There is something to be said for these joyous messengers
that we repel in our indignant orderliness.
They lift up the eyes, they lighten the heart,
and some day we'll decipher that sweet frenzied whistling
as they wheel and settle along our hard roofs
and take those grey buttresses for home.
One thing we know they say, after their fashion.
They like the warm cliffs of man.

King Billy

Grey over Riddrie the clouds piled up,
dragged their rain through the cemetery trees.
The gates shone cold. Wind rose
flaring the hissing leaves, the branches
swung, heavy, across the lamps.
Gravestones huddled in drizzling shadow,
flickering streetlight scanned the requiescats,
a name and an urn, a date, a dove
picked out, lost, half-regained.
What is this dripping wreath, blown from its grave
red, white, blue, and gold
'To Our Leader of Thirty Years Ago' –

Bareheaded, in dark suits, with flutes
and drums, they brought him here, in procession
seriously, King Billy of Brigton, dead,
from Bridgeton Cross: a memory of violence,
brooding days of empty bellies,
billiard smoke and a sour pint,
boots or fists, famous sherrickings,
the word, the scuffle, the flash, the shout,
bloody crumpling in the close,
bricks for papish windows, get
the Conks next time, the Conks ambush
the Billy Boys, the Billy Boys the Conks till
Sillitoe scuffs the razors down the stank –
No, but it isn't the violence they remember
but the legend of a violent man
born poor, gang-leader in the bad times
of idleness and boredom, lost in better days,
a bouncer in a betting club,
a quiet man at last, dying
alone in Bridgeton in a box bed.
So a thousand people stopped the traffic
for the hearse of a folk hero and the flutes
threw 'Onward Christian Soldiers' to the winds
from unironic lips, the mourners kept
in step, and there were some who wept.

Go from the grave. The shrill flutes
are silent, the march dispersed.
Deplore what is to be deplored,
and then find out the rest.

Glasgow Green

Clammy midnight, moonless mist.
A cigarette glows and fades on a cough.
Meth-men mutter on benches,
pawed by river fog. Monteith Row
sweats coldly, crumbles, dies
slowly. All shadows are alive.
Somewhere a shout's forced out – 'No!' –
it leads to nothing but silence,
except the whisper of the grass
and the other whispers that fill the shadows.

'What d'ye mean see me again?
D'ye think I came here jist for that?
I'm no finished with you yet.
I can get the boys t'ye, they're no that faur away.
You wouldny like that eh? Look there's no two ways aboot it.
Christ but I'm gaun to have you Mac
if it takes all night, turn over you bastard
turn over, I'll –'
                    Cut the scene.
Here there's no crying for help,
it must be acted out, again, again.

This is not the delicate nightmare
you carry to the point of fear
and wake from, it is life, the sweat
is real, the wrestling under a bush
is real, the dirty starless river
is the real Clyde, with a dishrag dawn
it rinses the horrors of the night
but cannot make them clean,

though washing blows
                    where the women watch
by day,
        and children run,
                        on Glasgow Green.

And how shall these men live?
Providence, watch them go!
Watch them love, and watch them die!
How shall the race be served?
It shall be served by anguish
as well as by children at play.
It shall be served by loneliness
as well as by family love.
It shall be served by hunter and hunted in their endless chain
as well as by those who turn back the sheets in peace.
The thorn in the flesh!
Providence, water it!
Do you think it is not watered?
Do you think it is not planted?
Do you think there is not a seed of the thorn
as there is also a harvest of the thorn?
Man, take in that harvest!
Help that tree to bear its fruit!
Water the wilderness, walk there, reclaim it!
Reclaim, regain, renew! Fill the barns and the vats!

Longing,
        longing
                shall find its wine.

Let the women sit in the Green
and rock their prams as the sheets
blow and whip in the sunlight.
But the beds of married love
are islands in a sea of desire.
Its waves break here, in this park,
splashing the flesh as it trembles
like driftwood through the dark.

In the Snack-bar

A cup capsizes along the formica,
slithering with a dull clatter.
A few heads turn in the crowded evening snack-bar.
An old man is trying to get to his feet
from the low round stool fixed to the floor.
Slowly he levers himself up, his hands have no power.
He is up as far as he can get. The dismal hump
looming over him forces his head down.
He stands in his stained beltless gaberdine
like a monstrous animal caught in a tent
in some story. He sways slightly,
the face not seen, bent down
in shadow under his cap.
Even on his feet he is staring at the floor
or would be, if he could see.
I notice now his stick, once painted white
but scuffed and muddy, hanging from his right arm.
Long blind, hunchback born, half paralysed
he stands
fumbling with the stick
and speaks:
'I want – to go to the – toilet.'

It is down two flights of stairs, but we go.
I take his arm. 'Give me – your arm – it's better,' he says.
Inch by inch we drift towards the stairs.
A few yards of floor are like a landscape
to be negotiated, in the slow setting out
time has almost stopped. I concentrate
my life to his: crunch of spilt sugar,
slidy puddle from the night's umbrellas,
table edges, people's feet,
hiss of the coffee-machine, voices and laughter,
smell of a cigar, hamburgers, wet coats steaming,
and the slow dangerous inches to the stairs.
I put his right hand on the rail
and take his stick. He clings to me. The stick
is in his left hand, probing the treads.
I guide his arm and tell him the steps.
And slowly we go down. And slowly we go down.

White tiles and mirrors at last. He shambles
uncouth into the clinical gleam.
I set him in position, stand behind him
and wait with his stick.
His brooding reflection darkens the mirror
but the trickle of his water is thin and slow,
an old man's apology for living.
Painful ages to close his trousers and coat –
I do up the last buttons for him.
He asks doubtfully, 'Can I – wash my hands?'
I fill the basin, clasp his soft fingers round the soap.
He washes, feebly, patiently. There is no towel.
I press the pedal of the drier, draw his hands
gently into the roar of the hot air.
But he cannot rub them together,
drags out a handkerchief to finish.
He is glad to leave the contraption, and face the stairs.
He climbs, and steadily enough.
He climbs, we climb. He climbs
with many pauses but with that one
persisting patience of the undefeated
which is the nature of man when all is said.
And slowly we go up. And slowly we go up.
The faltering, unfaltering steps
take him at last to the door
across that endless, yet not endless waste of floor.
I watch him helped on a bus. It shudders off in the rain.
The conductor bends to hear where he wants to go.

Wherever he could go it would be dark
and yet he must trust men.
Without embarrassment or shame
he must announce his most pitiful needs
in a public place. No one sees his face.
Does he know how frightening he is in his strangeness
under his mountainous coat, his hands like wet leaves
stuck to the half-white stick?
His life depends on many who would evade him.
But he cannot reckon up the chances,
having one thing to do,
to haul his blind hump through these rains of August.
Dear Christ, to be born for this!

33

Trio

Coming up Buchanan Street, quickly, on a sharp winter evening
a young man and two girls, under the Christmas lights –
The young man carries a new guitar in his arms,
the girl on the inside carries a very young baby,
and the girl on the outside carries a chihuahua.
And the three of them are laughing, their breath rises
in a cloud of happiness, and as they pass
the boy says, 'Wait till he sees this but!'
The chihuahua has a tiny Royal Stewart tartan coat like a teapot-
    holder,
the baby in its white shawl is all bright eyes and mouth like favours
    in a fresh sweet cake,
the guitar swells out under its milky plastic cover, tied at the neck
    with silver tinsel tape and a brisk sprig of mistletoe.
Orphean sprig! Melting baby! Warm chihuahua!
The vale of tears is powerless before you.
Whether Christ is born, or is not born, you
put paid to fate, it abdicates
                            under the Christmas lights.
Monsters of the year
go blank, are scattered back,
can't bear this march of three.

– And the three have passed, vanished in the crowd
(yet not vanished, for in their arms they wind
the life of men and beasts, and music,
laughter ringing them round like a guard)
at the end of this winter's day.

The Second Life

But does every man feel like this at forty –
I mean it's like Thomas Wolfe's New York, his
heady light, the stunning plunging canyons, beauty –
pale stars winking hazy downtown quitting-time,
and the winter moon flooding the skyscrapers, northern –
an aspiring place, glory of the bridges, foghorns
are enormous messages, a looming mastery
that lays its hand on the young man's bowels
until he feels in that air, that rising spirit
all things are possible, he rises with it
until he feels that he can never die –
Can it be like this, and is this what it means
in Glasgow now, writing as the aircraft roar
over building sites, in this warm west light
by the daffodil banks that were never so crowded and lavish –
green May, and the slow great blocks rising
under yellow tower cranes, concrete and glass and steel
out of a dour rubble it was and barefoot children gone –
Is it only the slow stirring, a city's renewed life
that stirs me, could it stir me so deeply
as May, but could May have stirred
what I feel of desire and strength
like an arm saluting a sun?

All January, all February the skaters
enjoyed Bingham's pond, the crisp cold evenings,
they swung and flashed among car headlights,
the drivers parked round the unlit pond
to watch them, and give them light, what laughter
and pleasure rose in the rare lulls
of the yards-away stream of wheels along Great Western Road!
The ice broke up, but the boats came out.
The painted boats are ready for pleasure.
The long light needs no headlamps.

Black oar cuts a glitter: it is heaven on earth.

Is it true that we come alive
not once, but many times?
We are drawn back to the image

of the seed in darkness, or the greying skin
of the snake that hides a shining one –
it will push that used-up matter off
and even the film of the eye is sloughed –
That the world may be the same, and we are not
and so the world is not the same,
the second eye is making again
this place, these waters and these towers,
they are rising again
as the eye stands up to the sun,
as the eye salutes the sun.

Many things are unspoken
in the life of a man, and with a place
there is an unspoken love also
in undercurrents, drifting, waiting its time.
A great place and its people are not renewed lightly.
The caked layers of grime
grow warm, like homely coats.
But yet they will be dislodged
and men will still be warm.
The old coats are discarded.
The old ice is loosed.
The old seeds are awake.

Slip out of darkness, it is time.

The Unspoken

When the troopship was pitching round the Cape
in '41, and there was a lull in the night uproar of seas and winds,
    and a sudden full moon
swung huge out of the darkness like the world it is,
and we all crowded onto the wet deck, leaning on the rail, our
    arms on each other's shoulders, gazing at the savage outcrop
    of great Africa,
And Tommy Cosh started singing 'Mandalay' and we joined in
    with our raucous chorus of the unforgettable song,

and the dawn came up like thunder like that moon drawing the
     water of our yearning
though we were going to war, and left us exalted,
that was happiness,
but it is not like that.

When the television newscaster said
the second sputnik was up, not empty
but with a small dog on board,
a half-ton treasury of life orbiting a thousand miles above the thin
     television masts and mists of November,
in clear space, heard, observed,
the faint far heartbeat sending back its message
steady and delicate,
and I was stirred by a deep confusion of feelings,
got up, stood with my back to the wall and my palms pressed
     hard against it, my arms held wide
as if I could spring from this earth –
not loath myself to go out that very day where Laika had shown
     man,
felt my cheeks burning with old Promethean warmth
rekindled – ready –
covered my face with my hands, seeing only an animal
strapped in a doomed capsule, but the future
was still there, cool and whole like the moon,
waiting to be taken, smiling even
as the dog's bones and the elaborate casket of aluminium
glow white and fuse in the arc of re-entry,
and I knew what I felt was history,
its thrilling brilliance came down,
came down,
comes down on us all, bringing pride and pity,
but it is not like that.

But Glasgow days and grey weathers, when the rain
beat on the bus shelter and you leaned slightly against me, and
     the back of your hand touched my hand in the shadows, and
     nothing was said,
when your hair grazed mine accidentally as we talked in a café,
     yet not quite accidentally,
when I stole a glance at your face as we stood in a doorway and
     found I was afraid

37

of what might happen if I should never see it again,
when we met, and met, in spite of such differences in our lives,
and did the common things that in our feeling
became extraordinary, so that our first kiss
was like the winter morning moon, and as you shifted in my arms
it was the sea changing the shingle that changes it
as if for ever (but we are bound by nothing, but like smoke
to mist or light in water we move, and mix) –
O then it was a story as old as war or man,
and although we have not said it we know it,
and although we have not claimed it we do it,
and although we have not vowed it we keep it,
without a name to the end.

From a City Balcony

How often when I think of you the day grows bright!
Our silent love
wanders in Glen Fruin with butterflies and cuckoos –
bring me the drowsy country thing! Let it drift above the traffic
by the open window with a cloud of witnesses –
a sparkling burn, white lambs, the blaze of gorse,
the cuckoos calling madly, the real white clouds over us,
white butterflies about your hand in the short hot grass,
and then the witness was my hand closing on yours,
my mouth brushing your eyelids and your lips
again and again till you sighed and turned for love.
Your breast and thighs were blazing like the gorse.
I covered your great fire in silence there.
We let the day grow old along the grass.
It was in the silence the love was.

Footsteps and witnesses! In this Glasgow balcony who pours
such joy like mountain water? It brims, it spills over and over
down to the parched earth and the relentless wheels.
How often will I think of you, until
our dying steps forget this light, forget
that we ever knew the happy glen,
or that I ever said, We must jump into the sun,
and we jumped into the sun.

When you go

When you go,
if you go,
and I should want to die,
there's nothing I'd be saved by
more than the time
you fell asleep in my arms
in a trust so gentle
I let the darkening room
drink up the evening, till
rest, or the new rain
lightly roused you awake.
I asked if you heard the rain in your dream
and half dreaming still you only said, I love you.

Strawberries

There were never strawberries
like the ones we had
that sultry afternoon
sitting on the step
of the open french window
facing each other
your knees held in mine
the blue plates in our laps
the strawberries glistening
in the hot sunlight
we dipped them in sugar
looking at each other
not hurrying the feast
for one to come
the empty plates
laid on the stone together
with the two forks crossed
and I bent towards you
sweet in that air
in my arms

abandoned like a child
from your eager mouth
the taste of strawberries
in my memory
lean back again
let me love you

let the sun beat
on our forgetfulness
one hour of all
the heat intense
and summer lightning
on the Kilpatrick hills

let the storm wash the plates

One Cigarette

No smoke without you, my fire.
After you left,
your cigarette glowed on in my ashtray
and sent up a long thread of such quiet grey
I smiled to wonder who would believe its signal
of so much love. One cigarette
in the non-smoker's tray.
As the last spire
trembles up, a sudden draught
blows it winding into my face.
Is it smell, is it taste?
You are here again, and I am drunk on your tobacco lips.
Out with the light.
Let the smoke lie back in the dark.
Till I hear the very ash
sigh down among the flowers of brass
I'll breathe, and long past midnight, your last kiss.

Absence

My shadow –
I woke to a wind swirling the curtains light and dark
and the birds twittering on the roofs, I lay cold
in the early light in my room high over London.
What fear was it that made the wind sound like a fire
so that I got up and looked out half-asleep
at the calm rows of street-lights fading far below?
Without fire
only the wind blew.
But in the dream I woke from, you
came running through the traffic, tugging me, clinging
to my elbow, your eyes spoke
what I could not grasp –
Nothing, if you were here!

The wind of the early quiet
merges slowly now with a thousand rolling wheels.
The lights are out, the air is loud.
It is an ordinary January day.
My shadow, do you hear the streets?
Are you at my heels? Are you here?
And I throw back the sheets.

In Sobieski's Shield

well the prophets were dancing in the end much
good it did them and the sun didn't rise at all
anywhere but we weren't among the frozen we had been
dematerialized the day before solar withdrawal
in a hurry it's true but by the best technique
who said only technique well anyhow the best
available and here we are now rematerialized
to the best of my knowledge on a minor planet
of a sun in Sobieski's Shield in our right mind I hope
approximately though not unshaken and admittedly
not precisely those who set out if one can
speak of it by that wellworn tellurian euphemism

41

in any case molecular reconstitution is no
sinecure even with mice and I wouldn't have been
utterly surprised if some of us had turned out
mice or worse

but at least not that or not yet the effects
of violent change are still slightly present an
indescribable stringent sensation like perhaps being
born or dying but no neither of these I am
very nearly who I was I see I have only
four fingers on my left hand and there's a sharp
twinge I never had in my knee and one most curious
I almost said birthmark and so it is in a sense
light brown shaped like a crazy heart spreading
across my right forearm well let it be we are
here my wife my son the rest of the laboratory
my wife has those streaks of fiery red in her
hair that is expected in women she looks very
frightened yet and lies rigid the rematerialization
is slow in her but that is probably better yes
her eyes flutter to mine questioning I nod can I
smile I think I can does she see me yes thank god
she is hardly altered apart from that extraordinarily
strange and beautiful crown of bright red hair
I draw her head into my arms and hide the sobbing
shuddering first breaths of her second life I don't
know what made me use that phrase who are we
if we are not who we were we have only
one life though we are huddled now in our
protective dome on this harsh metallic plain
that belches cobalt from its craters under a
white-bronze pulsing gong of a sun it was all
they could do for us light-years away it seemed suitable
dematerialization's impossible over short distances anyway
so let's start moving I can surely get onto my feet
yes hoy there

my son is staring fascinated at my four fingers
you've only one nipple I tell him and it's true
but for compensation when he speaks his boy's
treble has broken and at thirteen he is a man
what a limbo to lose childhood in where has

42

it gone between the throwing of a switch and these
alien iron hills across so many stars his blue eyes
are the same but there's a new graveness of the
second life that phrase again we go up together
to the concave of the dome the environment after all
has to be studied

is that a lake of mercury I can't quite see
through the smoke of the fumarole it's lifting now
but there's something puzzling even when I
my memory of mercury seems to be confused with
what is it blood no no mercury's not like blood
what then what is it I'm remembering or nearly
remembering look dad mercury he says and so it
must be but I see a shell-hole filled with rain-water
red in the sinking sun I know that landscape too
one of the wars far back twentieth century I think the
great war was it called France Flanders fields I remember
reading these craters waterlogged with rain mud blood
I can see a stark hand brandishing nothing through placid scum
in a lull of the guns what horror that the livid water
is not shaken by the pity of the tattoo on the dead arm
a heart still held above the despair of the mud
my god the heart on my arm my second birth mark
the rematerialization has picked up these fragments I have
a graft of war and ancient agony forgive
me my dead helper

the sulky pool of mercury stares back at me I am
seeing normally now but I know these flashes will return
from the far past times I gather my wife and son to me
with a fierce gesture that surprises them I am not
a demonstrative man yet how to tell them
what and who I am that we are bound to all that lived
though the barriers are unspeakable we know a little of that
but something what is it gets through it is not
an essence but an energy how it pierces how it
clutches for still as I run my hand through her
amazing hair streaming on my shoulder I feel
a fist shaken in a shell-hole turn in my very marrow
we shall live in the rings of this chain the jeremiahs
who said nothing human would stand are confounded if I cry

43

even the dry tear in my heart that I cannot
stop or if I laugh to think they thought they
could divide the indivisible the old moon's in
the new moon's arms let's take our second
like our first life out from the dome are the suits
ready the mineral storm is quieter it's hard
to go let's go

From the Domain of Arnheim

And so that all these ages, these years
we cast behind us, like the smoke-clouds
dragged back into vacancy when the rocket springs –

The domain of Arnheim was all snow, but we were there.
We saw a yellow light thrown on the icefield
from the huts by the pines, and laughter came up
floating from a white corrie
miles away, clearly.
We moved on down, arm in arm.
I know you would have thought it was a dream
but we were there. And those were trumpets –
tremendous round the rocks –
while they were burning fires of trash and mammoths' bones.
They sang naked, and kissed in the smoke.
A child, or one of their animals, was crying.
Young men blew the ice crystals off their drums.
We came down among them, but of course
they could see nothing, on their time-scale.
Yet they sensed us, stopped, looked up – even into our eyes.
To them we were a displacement of the air,
a sudden chill, yet we had no power
over their fear. If one of them had been dying
he would have died. The crying
came from one just born: that was the cause
of the song. We saw it now. What had we stopped
but joy?
I know you felt
the same dismay, you gripped my arm, they were waiting
for what they knew of us to pass.

A sweating trumpeter took
a brand from the fire with a shout and threw it
where our bodies would have been –
we felt nothing but his courage.
And so they would deal with every imagined power
seen or unseen.
There are no gods in the domain of Arnheim.

We signalled to the ship; got back;
our lives and days returned to us, but
haunted by deeper souvenirs than any rocks or seeds.
From time the souvenirs are deeds.

What is 'Paradise Lost' really *about*?

The bard has fired his bullet at the fox.
The dilatory fox is full of duck.
The gun takes brush and breakfast, quack and cluck.
Foxes in satchels are sequestered flocks.

The critic takes the satchel with a cry.
'Your fur is feathers! You have bagged a bird!'
The simple bard is bolshy when he's stirred.
'I felled a fox, and foxes cannot fly.'

Deep in the duck the maggot faintly mauls.
Viruses mill within the maggot's vein.
The photomicrograph shows fields of grain.
Down in these fields the fox's double falls.

Critics can pant across this paradox.
Critics can call the bard a blunderbuss.
Bards who have shot their shout are boisterous.
Bards have the fox's body in a box.

45

A View of Things

what I love about dormice is their size
what I hate about rain is its sneer
what I love about the Bratach Gorm is its unflappability
what I hate about scent is its smell
what I love about newspapers is their etaoin shrdl
what I hate about philosophy is its pursed lip
what I love about Rory is his old grouse
what I hate about Pam is her pinkie
what I love about semi-precious stones is their preciousness
what I hate about diamonds is their mink
what I love about poetry is its ion engine
what I hate about hogs is their setae
what I love about love is its porridge-spoon
what I hate about hate is its eyes
what I love about hate is its salts
what I hate about love is its dog
what I love about Hank is his string vest
what I hate about the twins is their three gloves
what I love about Mabel is her teeter
what I hate about gooseberries is their look, feel, smell, and taste
what I love about the world is its shape
what I hate about a gun is its lock, stock, and barrel
what I love about bacon-and-eggs is its predictability
what I hate about derelict buildings is their reluctance to
    disintegrate
what I love about a cloud is its unpredictability
what I hate about you, chum, is your china
what I love about many waters is their inability to quench love

Phoning

The roofs and cranes
and the dark rain

I look back
remembering an evening
we sat on the bed
and I dialled Montreux
a sudden impulse
we had to laugh
at that chain of numbers
0104121615115
Grand Hôtel des Alpes
and we spoke to your sister
Glasgow to the snows
and the sunny funiculars
and meetings by a lake
so far from Law and
the pits and cones
of worked Lanarkshire
my arm on your shoulder
held you as you spoke
your voice vibrating
as you leaned against me
remembering this
and your finger tapping
my bare knee
to emphasize a point
but most of all
in that dusky room
the back of your head
as you bent to catch
the distant words
caught my heart
vulnerable
as the love
with which I make
this sunset chain
remembering

deep in the city
far from the snows

The Flowers of Scotland

Yes, it is too cold in Scotland for flower people; in any case who
would be handed a thistle?
What are our flowers? Locked swings and private rivers –
and the island of Staffa for sale in the open market, which no one
questions or thinks strange –
and lads o' pairts that run to London and Buffalo without a back-
ward look while their elders say Who'd blame them –
and bonny fechters kneedeep in dead ducks with all the thrawn
intentness of the incorrigible professional Scot –
and a Kirk Assembly that excels itself in the bad old rhetoric and
tries to stamp out every glow of charity and change, most
wrong when it thinks most loudly it is most right –
and a Scottish National Party that refuses to discuss Vietnam and
is even applauded for doing so, do they think no lesson is to
be learned from what is going on there? –
and the unholy power of Grouse-moor and Broad-acres to
prevent the smoke of useful industry from sullying Inver-
gordon or setting up linear cities among the whaups –
and the banning of Beardsley and Joyce but not of course of
'Monster on the Campus' or 'Curse of the Undead' – those
who think the former are the more degrading, what are their
values?
and the steady creep of the preservationist societies, wearing their
pens out for slums with good leaded lights – if they could buy
all the amber in the Baltic and melt it over Edinburgh would
they be happy then? – the skeleton is well-proportioned –
and by contrast the massive indifference to the slow death of the
Clyde estuary, decline of resorts, loss of steamers, anaemia of
yachting, cancer of monstrous installations of a foreign power
and an acquiescent government – what is the smell of death
on a child's spade, any more than rats to leaded lights? –
and dissidence crying in the wilderness to a moor of boulders
and two ospreys –
these are the flowers of Scotland.

1969

Instamatic Poems

GLASGOW 5 MARCH 1971

With a ragged diamond
of shattered plate-glass
a young man and his girl
are falling backwards into a shop-window.
The young man's face
is bristling with fragments of glass
and the girl's leg has caught
on the broken window
and spurts arterial blood
over her wet-look white coat.
Their arms are starfished out
braced for impact,
their faces show surprise, shock,
and the beginning of pain.
The two youths who have pushed them
are about to complete the operation
reaching into the window
to loot what they can smartly.
Their faces show no expression.
It is a sharp clear night
in Sauchiehall Street.
In the background two drivers
keep their eyes on the road.

VENICE APRIL 1971

Three black gondolas
cut the sparkle of the lagoon.

In the first, the Greek archimandrite
stands, a young black-bearded man
in gold cope, black hood, black shoulder veil blown back
in the sunny breeze. In front of him
his even younger acolyte holds high
the glittering processional cross. His long black robe

glitters with delicious silver flowers
against the blue of the sky.

In the second gondola Stravinsky goes.
The black fringe trails the lapping water,
the heavy coffin dips the golden lions on the sides,
the gondoliers are ankle-deep in roses,
the coffin sways crowned with roses,
the gondoliers' white blouses and black sashes
startle their brown arms, the shining oars,
the pink and crimson flowers.

And the third gondola
is like a shadow
where the widow goes.

And there at the edge of the picture
where the crowds cross themselves
and weep a little in the Italian way,
an old poet with white hair
and hooded, piercing eyes
leans on his stick
and without expression
watches the boats move out
from his shore.

MOUGINS PROVENCE SEPTEMBER 1971

A picture of a picture of a picture.
Sort out the splendid lights.
A parrot with crusty eye
flutters on the curtain-rail, kimonos
on hooks, bullfighters' skintight suits
blaze. Liquid
Dufys, Matisses in fauve stacks,
an Afghan hound in the real autumn sunlight, veranda
geraniums, geraniums on palettes on chairs,
wet canvases drowning in vandyke brown.
A sunburnt leprechaun of eighty-nine
in flowered shirt and shorts

twinkles a borrowed Pentax at his wife
and waves at the real photographer a sketch
of the artist at his easel sketching
his model in the morning of life.
His Spanish eyes are merry as chestnuts.
The interviewer holds his breath.

GLASGOW NOVEMBER 1971

The 'speckled pipe' of the MacCrimmons,
three centuries old, is being played
in a backcourt very far from Dunvegan.
A young director of the College of Piping
is trying it out for a radio programme.
Only his cheeks show the pibroch
that rises winding into the wintry city air.
It is the long drones that are speckled,
carved in clusters of elegant bands
of creamy horn and dark brown wood,
but speckled are the high tenement walls behind them,
dark stone, pale mortar, narrow verticals
of dark window and water-pipe and pale smudge of curtains,
and speckled is the piper's kilt
against a speckled homely jungle
of grasses, thistles, dandelions, fireweed, firewood,
Capstan packets and Lanliq empties.
In a camouflage the pibroch
and the pibroch-player
disappear, half appear
MacCrimmons in Hornel.

LONDON NOVEMBER 1971

At the Festival of Islam
the dervishes are dancing.
The dancemaster stands
in his long black gown

51

straight-backed, his hands
folded in front of him.
Twelve swarthy men
in cylindrical hats
and loose white blouses
and long white skirts
and their long white sleeves
stretched out straight
like the albatross
have begun to dance.
The drum measures
flutes and strings
and men following.
Serious, rapt,
as if to wind themselves
up with their arms
they revolve, their skirts
flaring out loose
in white pyramids
below the inverted
pyramids of white
blouses and arms
which support the top
truncated pyramids
of circling hats.
Pattern and no pattern,
alone and in union
without unison
in the hard light
of Friends' House
in Euston Road
the dervishes whirl
round, they dance
round, round
they go, without
sound, now,
round and round.

DONA EMA BRAZIL APRIL 1972

In a cabin of sweet cedarwood
deep in an orange-grove
an old Hungarian doctor-poet, dying,
is writing his last quirky postcard
to an English friend. His brown eyes twinkle
as he thinks of his thirteen languages,
his theory of pain, his use of hypnosis
in childbirth, his work with the Resistance
in Italy, his wryest fame in *Winnie*
Ille Pu, his end
in a nest of lianas.
With a laugh he stops
just short of the date
which who cares who will add.
ALEXANDER LENARD, says the card,
obiit, meghalt, starb, mori, died.

BRADFORD JUNE 1972

Dusty, bruised and grazed, and cut about a bit, but
cheerful, twenty men in white
are demolishing an old stone house
by karate.
They attack the worst part:
the thick cemented fireplace wall.
What a concert of chops is conducted
by him in the helmet, with KARATE INSTRUCTOR
across his back and Union Jacks and ideograms
along his sleeve: a deep-breathed plot
of timed and buttressed energies jabbing
one bare hand and two bare hands and
one bare foot and two bare feet and
one bare head at
stone: the pivot man,
swarming with badges, swings
on two friends' shoulders, clutches
their necks, leans back with knees

above his head and like a spring
uncoils two smart sharp whacks
from heels of steel,
and the wall keels.

DARMSTADT SEPTEMBER 1972

A middle-aged precision instrument mechanic
having fallen behind with the mortgage repayments
on a fine new house, has kitted up
the workbench in his study
with a home-made, but well-made
guillotine, the blade
a nicely slicing two-feet-long steel
paper-trimmer, the weight
a tested squat steel
anvil, the complex of ropes
designed to release the trimmer
with a perfectly shimmering swish of
descent on the neck as he lies
prone on the bench, and
like a precision instrument
he has pulled the rope
so delicately that his head,
though severed, sits still
on the board. It looks straight
at his wife standing in the door.

GLASGOW OCTOBER 1972

At the Old Ship Bank pub in Saltmarket
a milk-lapping contest is in progress.
A dozen very assorted Bridgeton cats
have sprung from their starting-blocks
to get their heads down in the gleaming saucers.
In the middle of the picture

young Tiny is about to win his bottle of whisky
by kittening through the sweet half-gill
in one minute forty seconds flat, but
Sarah, at the end of the line,
self-contained and silver-grey,
has sat down with her back to the saucer
and surveys the photographers calmly.
She is a cat who does not like milk.

ANDES MOUNTAINS DECEMBER 1972

FUERZA AEREA URUG —
nothing more can be read on the fuselage,
tailless, wingless, a jagged cylinder
at rest in a wilderness of snow and rock.
A rugby charter from Montevideo,
the Old Christians and their supporters.
Two months after the crash, it would not seem
a bleak scene
as the sixteen tough surviving young Old Christians
crouch in the mouth of the cylinder,
sipping cups of melted snow and cherry wine,
eating quickly from plastic air force plates,
but for the yellow hands
and feet all round them
in the snow, and skulls. The plane's
fire-axe stands in today's body. The shell
where the sweet brain had been is scooped clean.
Razors have flayed the limbs in strips.
A dozen of the dead
have played their part, a dozen more
are laid out, snow-packed, in neat rows
like fish in a box. Cherry wine and blood
are as one on their chins as the flesh
they bless becomes Old Christians.

LONDON JANUARY 1973

It is not a pile of diamonds,
it is not tons of money
that lie like a deadweight over gemsman Julius Beer.
His hideous mausoleum in Highgate Cemetery,
revealed in this journalist's flash,
is a pit of filth half filled
with pigeon-droppings and dead pigeons and
pigeons dying hundredweight on hundredweight
trapped in that poisonous cote.
Down through the broken wire of the cupola
they come, but cannot fly back out.
One flutters weakly at the top of the picture,
will soon fall into gehenna.
In the diamondman's invisible bones
nothing takes root but death.

Columba's Song

Where's Brude? Where's Brude?
So many souls to be saved!
The bracken is thick, the wildcat is quick,
the foxes dance in the moonlight,
the salmon dance in the waters,
the adders dance in the thick brown bracken.
Where's Brude? Where's man?
There's too much nature here,
eagles and deer,
but where's the mind and where's the soul?
Show me your kings, your women, the man of the plough.
And cry me to your cradles.
It wasn't for a fox or an eagle I set sail!

Floating off to Timor

If only we'd been strangers
we'd be floating off to Timor,
we'd be shimmering on the Trades
in a blue jersey boat
with shandies, flying-fish,
a pace of dolphins
to the copra ports.
And it's no use crying
to me, What dolphins?
I know where they are
and I'd have snapped you up
and carried you away
snapped you up
and carried you away
if we had been strangers.

But here we are care
of the back roofs.
It's not hard to find
with a collar turned up

and a hoot from the Clyde.
The steps come home
whistling too. And a kettle
steams the cranes out slowly.
It's living with ships
makes a rough springtime
and who is safe
when they sing and blow
their music – they seem
to swing at some light rope
like those desires
we keep for strangers.
God, the yellow deck
breathes, it heaves spray
back like a shout.
We're cutting through
some straits of the world
in our old dark room
with salty wings
in the shriek of the dock wind.
But we're caught – meshed
in the fish-scales, ferries,
mudflats, lifebelts
fading into football cries
and the lamps coming on
to bring us in.

We take in
the dream, a cloth from the line
the trains fling sparks on
in our city. We're better awake.
But you know I'd take
you all the same,
if you were my next stranger.

In Glasgow

In my smoochy corner
take me on a cloud
I'll wrap you round
and lay you down
in smoky tinfoil
rings and records
sheets of whisky
and the moon all right
old pal all right
the moon all night

Mercy for the rainy
tyres and the violet
thunder that bring you
shambling and shy
from chains of Easterhouse
plains of lights
make your delight
in my nest my spell
my arms and my shell
my barn my bell

I've combed your hair
and washed your feet
and made you turn
like a dark eel
in my white bed
till morning lights
a silent cigarette
throw on your shirt
I lie staring yet
forget forget

The Apple's Song

Tap me with your finger,
rub me with your sleeve,
hold me, sniff me, peel me
curling round and round
till I burst out white and cold
from my tight red coat
and tingle in your palm
as if I'd melt and breathe
a living pomander
waiting for the minute
of joy when you lift me
to your mouth and crush me
and in taste and fragrance
I race through your head
in my dizzy dissolve.

I sit in the bowl
in my cool corner
and watch you as you pass
smoothing your apron.
Are you thirsty yet?
My eyes are shining.

The Woman

A string of pearls
in the dark window, that wet spring,
sometimes a white hand raised with a cigarette
blurred by rain and buses
anyhow. A lonely
ring.

Nothing she was waiting for
came, unless what took her
in the coldest arms.

It seems to be the pearls
we remember, for what they spoke
of another life than waiting,
and being unknown dying
in a high dark street.

Who she was you'll keep thinking.
The hearse rolled off in thunder,
but showers only lay dust.

At the Television Set

Take care if you kiss me,
you know it doesn't die.
The lamplight reaches out, draws it
blandly – all of it – into fixity,
troops of blue shadows like the soundless gunfight,
yellow shadows like your cheek by the lamp
where you lie watching, half watching
between the yellow and the blue.
I half see you, half know you.
Take care if you turn now to face me.
For even in this room we are moving out through stars
and forms that never let us back, your hand
lying lightly on my thigh and my hand on your shoulder
are transfixed only there, not here.

What can you bear that would last
like a rock through cancer and white hair?

Yet it is not easy
to take stock of miseries
when the soft light flickers
along our arms in the stillness
where decisions are made.
You have to look at me,
and then it's time that falls
talking slowly to sleep.

For Bonfires

I

The leaves are gathered, the trees are dying
for a time.
A seagull cries through white smoke in the garden fires
that fill the heavy air.
All day heavy air
is burning, a moody dog
sniffs and circles the swish of the rake.
In streaks of ash, the gardener drifting
ghostly, beats his hands, a cloud
of breath to the red sun.

II

An island in the city, happy demolition men
behind windowed hoardings – look at them
trailing drills through rubble dust, kicking rubble,
smoking leaning on a pick, putting the stub
over an ear and the hot yellow helmet over that,
whistling up the collapsing chimney, kicking the
ricochet, rattling the trail with
snakes of wire, slamming slabs
down, plaster, cornice, brick, brick
on broken brick and plaster dust,
sprawling with steaming cans and pieces
at noon, afternoon bare sweat shining
paths down chalky backs, coughing
in filtered sunshine, slithering, swearing,
joking, slowly stacking and building
their rubbish into a total bonfire.
Look at that Irishman, bending
in a beautiful arc to throw
the last black rafter to the top,
stands back, walks round it singing
as it crackles into flame – old doors,
old beams, boxes, window-frames,
a rag doll, sacks, flex, old newspapers,
burst shelves, a shoe, old dusters, rags of
wallpaper roses. And they all stand round,
and cheer the tenement to smoke.

III

In a galvanized bucket
the letters burn. They roar and twist
and the leaves curl back one by one.
They put out claws and scrape the iron
like a living thing,
but the scrabbling to be free soon subsides.
The black pages fuse
to a single whispering mass
threaded by dying tracks of gold.
Let them grow cold,
and when they're dead
quickly draw breath.

Blue Toboggans

scarves for the apaches
wet gloves for snowballs
whoops for white clouds
and blue toboggans

stamping for a tingle
lamps for four o'clock
steamed glass for buses
and blue toboggans

tuning-forks for Wenceslas
white fogs for Prestwick
mince pies for the Eventides
and blue toboggans

TV for the lonely
a long haul for heaven
a shilling for the gas
and blue toboggans

Lord Jim's Ghost's Tiger Poem

I can see them yet round the bungalow,
queuing up swaying and groaning slightly,
each to his steaming bowl as we had taught them –
tigers with a taste for tea were all
the rage that year at the Monsoon Club.

There was an old glade of tombs we went to
every rainy season to renew
our stock of ghosts, once brought back a rice doll,
grew into a fine peasant boy, kept our accounts –
said the old ghost in the Monsoon Club.

Lying on the rattan with pipes glowing
we saw a bird of paradise in paradise
bending to its image in an image
until a rain of diamonds was rain –
pattering white on the Monsoon Club.

The fishes in the river were choked with rice
when we came down, came down with our hooks
and threw them all back, our bottles slung
at our hips and the slurred fish sutra on our lips –
rowing back dark to the Monsoon Club.

And velvet cobras took smoke apart.
And the flute climbed above its notes.
And backs took the needle for blue tigers.
And the dead whistled through a tin sheet.
And we played go at the Monsoon Club.

Go and opium and rain! Bead-curtains
spilling round naked breasts like water!
Thunder and lacquer! All gone like that mist
framed by early morning summer doors,
my drowsy morning Monsoon Club.

I hear the slow pagoda bell.
I smell the salt of the China Sea.
I trace with the glow of my cigarette
in my hammock swinging through the straits
letters of smoke – Monsoon Club.

Hyena

I am waiting for you.
I have been travelling all morning through the bush
and not eaten.
I am lying at the edge of the bush
on a dusty path that leads from the burnt-out kraal.
I am panting, it is midday, I found no water-hole.
I am very fierce without food and although my eyes
are screwed to slits against the sun
you must believe I am prepared to spring.

What do you think of me?
I have a rough coat like Africa.
I am crafty with dark spots
like the bush-tufted plains of Africa.
I sprawl as a shaggy bundle of gathered energy
like Africa sprawling in its waters.
I trot, I lope, I slaver, I am a ranger.
I hunch my shoulders. I eat the dead.

Do you like my song?
When the moon pours hard and cold on the veldt
I sing, and I am the slave of darkness.
Over the stone walls and the mud walls and the ruined places
and the owls, the moonlight falls.
I sniff a broken drum. I bristle. My pelt is silver.
I howl my song to the moon – up it goes.
Would you meet me there in the waste places?

It is said I am a good match
for a dead lion. I put my muzzle
at his golden flanks, and tear. He
is my golden supper, but my tastes are easy.
I have a crowd of fangs, and I use them.
Oh and my tongue – do you like me
when it comes lolling out over my jaw
very long, and I am laughing?
I am not laughing.
But I am not snarling either, only
panting in the sun, showing you
what I grip
carrion with.

I am waiting
for the foot to slide,
for the heart to seize,
for the leaping sinews to go slack,
for the fight to the death to be fought to the death,
for a glazing eye and the rumour of blood.
I am crouching in my dry shadows
till you are ready for me.
My place is to pick you clean
and leave your bones to the wind.

The Loch Ness Monster's Song

Sssnnnwhuffffll?
Hnwhuffl hhnnwfl hnfl hfl?
Gdroblboblhobngbl gbl gl g g g g glbgl.
Drublhaflablhaflubhafgabhaflhafl fl fl –
gm grawwwww grf grawf awfgm graw gm.
Hovoplodok-doplodovok-plovodokot-doplodokosh?
Splgraw fok fok splgrafhatchgabrlgabrl fok splfok!
Zgra kra gka fok!
Grof grawff gahf?
Gombl mbl bl –
blm plm,
blm plm,
blm plm,
blp.

Afterwards

Afterwards the sun shone on seven rice shoots and a black tree.

Afterwards the prostitutes fell on lean times / some took up embroidery / one became a pearl-diver and was drowned.

Afterwards my burned little cousin went through eleven grafting operations / never cried.

Afterwards many saffron robes began to be let out / there was a movement to purify the order.

Afterwards the ancient monuments were restored stone by stone / I thought it was folly when I saw the list of legless girls waiting for prosthetic appliances.

Afterwards there was a report of mass ghosts on the plains, all grey as dust, with grey shovels, burying and burying all through the night to the beat of a drum / but in the morning the earth was hard and unbroken.

Afterwards came six great harvests and a glut of fish, and the rivers rolled and steamed through tunnels of fresh green fruit-trees and lilypads needled by kingfishers / rainbow after rainbow plunged into the lakes of rice.

Afterwards I went out with my sister one still hot day into the forest, and we came to an old temple bombed to a shell, with weeds in its windows, and went hand in hand through a deep rubble of stone and fragments of half-melted statues and rubbish of metal and flowers and bread, and there in a corner we saw the skeleton of a boy, with shreds of blue cotton clinging to the bones, his fingers still clutching the string of a tiny bamboo box / we bent down as a faint chirping started from the box, and saw that it was his grass-hopper, alive yet and scraping the only signal it knew from behind the bars of its cage / you said something and burst out crying / I slid the latch then and set it free.

Thoughts of a Module

It is black so. There is that dust.
My ladder in light. What are my men.
One is foot down. That is pack drill.
Black what is vizor. A hiss I heard.
The talks go up. Clump now but float.
Is a jump near. A camera paced out.
I phase another man. Another man is second.
Second last feet on. The dust I think.
So some soles cross. Is a flag near.
No move yon flag. Which voice comes down.
White house thanks all. Command module man not.
Is kangaroo hop around. I think moon dance.
Or white bird is. Good oxygen I heard.
Earth monitors must be. Is it too pressing.
Trained man is gay. Fail safe is gay.
The black I see. What instruments are lonely.
Sharp is a shadow. A horizon goes flat.
All rock are samples. Dust taken I think.
Is bright my leg. In what sun yonder.
An end I think. How my men go.
The talks come down. The ladder I shake.
To leave that bright. Space dark I see.
Is my men last. Men are that first.
That moon is here. They have some dust.
Is home they know. Blue earth I think.
I lift I see. It is that command.
My men go back. I leave that here.
It is bright so.

The First Men on Mercury

– We come in peace from the third planet.
Would you take us to your leader?

– Bawr stretter! Bawr. Bawr. Stretterhawl?

– This is a little plastic model
of the solar system, with working parts.
You are here and we are there and we
are now here with you, is this clear?

– Gawl horrop. Bawr. Abawrhannahanna!

– Where we come from is blue and white
with brown, you see we call the brown
here 'land', the blue is 'sea', and the white
is 'clouds' over land and sea, we live
on the surface of the brown land,
all round is sea and clouds. We are 'men'.
Men come –

– Glawp men! Gawrbenner menko. Menhawl?

– Men come in peace from the third planet
which we call 'earth'. We are earthmen.
Take us earthmen to your leader.

– Thmen? Thmen? Bawr. Bawrhossop.
Yuleeda tan hanna. Harrabost yuleeda.

– I am the yuleeda. You see my hands,
we carry no benner, we come in peace.
The spaceways are all stretterhawn.

– Glawn peacemen all horrabhanna tantko!
Tan come at'mstrossop. Glawp yuleeda!

– Atoms are peacegawl in our harraban.
Menbat worrabost from tan hannahanna.

– You men we know bawrhossoptant. Bawr.
We know yuleeda. Go strawg backspetter quick.

– We cantantabawr, tantingko backspetter now!

– Banghapper now! Yes, third planet back.
Yuleeda will go back blue, white, brown
nowhanna! There is no more talk.

– Gawl han fasthapper?

– No. You must go back to your planet.
Go back in peace, take what you have gained
but quickly.

– Stretterworra gawl, gawl . . .

– Of course, but nothing is ever the same,
now is it? You'll remember Mercury.

Spacepoem 3: Off Course

the golden flood   the weightless seat
the cabin song   the pitch black
the growing beard   the floating crumb
the shining rendezvous   the orbit wisecrack
the hot spacesuit   the smuggled mouth-organ
the imaginary somersault   the visionary sunrise
the turning continents   the space debris
the golden lifeline   the space walk
the crawling deltas   the camera moon
the pitch velvet   the rough sleep
the crackling headphone   the space silence
the turning earth   the lifeline continents
the cabin sunrise   the hot flood
the shining spacesuit   the growing moon
    the crackling somersault   the smuggled orbit
    the rough moon   the visionary rendezvous

70

the weightless headphone   the cabin debris
the floating lifeline   the pitch sleep
the crawling camera   the turning silence
the space crumb   the crackling beard
the orbit mouth-organ   the floating song

Itinerary

i

We went to Oldshoremore.
Is the Oldshoremore road still there?
You mean the old shore road?
I suppose it's more an old road than a shore road.
No more! They shored it up, but it's washed away.
So you could sing the old song –
Yes we sang the old song:
    We'll take the old Oldshoremore shore road no more.

ii

We passed the Muckle Flugga.
Did you see the muckle flag?
All we saw was the muckle fog.
The flag says ULTIMA FLUGGA WHA'S LIKE US.
Couldn't see flag for fug, sorry.
Ultimately –
    Ultimately we made for Muck and flogged the lugger.

iii

Was it bleak at Bowhousebog?
It was black as a hoghouse, boy.
Yes, but bleak?
Look, it was black as a bog and bleak as the Bauhaus!
The Bauhaus wasn't black –
Will you get off my back!
So there were dogs too?
    Dogs, hogs, leaks in the bogs – we never went back.

71

Not Playing the Game

– Although a poem is
undoubtedly a 'game'
it is not a game.
And although now it is even
part of the game to say so,
making it a "'game'"
is spooky, and we'll
not play that.

– Who are you kidding, said
the next card. You just played.

– Anything I play
has no rules, if
you see the rules
it's only 'play' –
the 'dealer's eyeshade'.

– I like that smoker's cough the "'dealer's eyeshade'".
Your deal is showing, my dear.

– Back in the box you go in words.
'Back in the box', in other words.
Now we'll just let that
""'dealer's eyeshade'""
wilt on whatever can support it, like
a poem on baize.

Rider

i

a grampus whacked the hydrophone / Loch Fyne left its green
      bed, fled / shrieking to Cowal / it all began
the nutcracker closed round Port Glasgow / it snapped with a
      burst of docks and / capstans downwind like collarstuds
cabbage whites in deadlock / were hanged from geans and
      rowans / wedlock-red
Greenock in steam / hammered albatrosses onto packingcases /
      without forgiveness / zam
by the waters of Glasgow / angels hung pilgrims, primroses,
      Dante, black blankets / over and over / the acid streams
a giant hedgehog lifting the Necropolis / solid silver / to the
      moon / sang of the deluge
long keys of gas unlocked the shaking Campsies at / last, at
      least / four drumlins were heard howling / as far as Fenwick
      Moor
Calderpark was sucked into a belljar, came out / at Kalgoorlie
      with elephants and northern lights
ravening taxis roasted dogs in basements, basted / chicken
      wheels in demolition oil / slept by the swing / of the
      wrecker's ball
the Holy Loch turned to granite chips, the ships / died with their
      stiff upper lips reaching to Aviemore
Para Handy sculled through the subway with the Stone of
      Destiny / shot the rapids at Cessnock right into Sunday
      morning
a coelacanth on stilts was setting fire to Sauchiehall Street when
      Tom Leonard /
sold James B. V. Thomson a horse, black /
in the night and dust / which galloped him away /
deep as the grave / writing

ii

Davidson looked through the telescope at MacDiarmid and said /
      what, is that God
Davidson rode off on a blood-splashed stag / into the sea /
      horses ultimately
Davidson sold / fish to Neptune, fire / to Prometheus, to him-
      self / a prisoner's iron bed, the red

73

sun rose flapping slowly over Nietzsche / bars melted into
    sand / black marias stalled in Calton
the rainbow dropped its pot of lead on Peterhead / the peter keys
    were blown to breadcrumbs, fed
to men forbid / the men bought lead, built jails, went mad, lay
    dead / in iron fields
the jaws of Nero smouldered in a dustbin / cinders tingled / the
    dead rose / tamam
sulphur shoes dancing to Mars / their zircon eyeshades flashed,
    beryllium / toeguards clipped Mercury's boulders
Lucretius was found lying under the flary walls / of a universe
    in the Crab nebula / crying
the dancers brought him water / where he lay he rose, froze / in
    a mandala like a flame / blessing
the darkness of all disbelievers / filaments of the Crab wrapped
    him in hydrogen shroud / remade
he walked by Barrhead and Vauxhall Bridge, by the sea waited /
    with his dark horse in the dangerous night air
for a rider / his testament
delivered to the earth, kicking /
the roots of things

iii
five hundred million hummingbirds sat in the Kelvin Hall / three
    hundred thousand girls took double basses
in a crocodile to Inverkip / six thousand children drew Rothesay
    through twelve thousand kites / two hundred
plumbers with morning cellos galvanized the bedmakers of
    Fairlie / forty babies
threw their teething-rings at a helicopter / trickety-track / till
    Orpheus looked back
and there was nothing but the lonely hills and sky unless the
    chilling wind was something / and the space
of pure white pain where his wife had held his hand from hell /
    he left the place
and came to a broken shack at midday / with carts and horses /
    strong dark ragged boys
played in the smoke / the gypsies gave him soup and bread / for
    the divine brooch / who cares
what is divine, he said / and passed into the valley of the Clyde,
    a cloud / followed

and many campfires in that landscape, dogs whining, cuckoos,
　　glasshouses, thundershowers /
David Gray shook the rain from his hair and held his heart, the
　　Luggie flashed
in the lightning of the last March storm / he led a sweet brown
　　mare into the mist / the apple-boughs
closed over, where the flute
of Orpheus was only wished for /
in the drip of trees

iv
butcher-boys tried to ward off sharks / the waters rose quickly /
　　great drowned bankers
floated from bay-windows / two housemaids struggled on
　　Grosvenor Terrace with a giant conger
the Broomielaw was awash with slime and torn-out claws and
　　anchor-flakes / rust and dust
sifted together where a dredger ploughed up the Gallowgate /
　　pushed a dirty wave over Shettleston
spinning shopfronts crashed in silence / glassily, massively /
　　porticoes tilting / settled in mud
lampreys fastened on four dead sailors drifting through Finnieston
　　/ in a Drygate attic
James Macfarlan threw his pen at the stinking wall / the whisky
　　and the stinking poverty
ran down like ink / the well of rats was bottomless and Scotch /
　　the conman and the conned
fought on / the ballads yellowed, the pubs filled / at Anderston
　　he reached his grave in snow / selah
the ruined cities were switched off / there was no flood / his father
　　led a pedlar's horse
by Carrick fields, his mother sang / the boy rode on a jogging
　　back / far back / in rags /
Dixon's Blazes roared and threw more poets in its molten pools /
　　forges on fire
matched the pitiless bread, the head
long hangdog, the lifted elbow /
the true bloody pathos and sublime

v

Kossuth took a coalblack horse from Debrecen / clattered up
    Candleriggs into the City Hall
three thousand cheers could never drown the groaning fortress-
    bars / a thousand years
heard the wind howl / scimitars, eagles, bugles, edicts, whips,
    crowns, in the pipes / playing / the grave plain in the sun
handcuffed keelies shouted in Albion Street / slogans in red
    fragments broke the cobblestones, Kossuth
drew a mirage on electric air / the hare sat calmly on the door-
    step / it was Monday over all the world / om
Tom McGrath mixed bread and milk for the young hare / Monk
    and Parker spoke in a corner / the still room
was taken / Dougal Graham stood on his hands, the bell / rang
    between his feet / he rolled
on his hump through the swarming Tontine piazzas, swam / in
    dogs, parcels, puddles, tobacco-quids
ran with a bawbee ballad five feet long / felt fishwives / gutted
    a brace of Glasgow magistrates / lay
with a pig in his arms and cried the city fathers bitches / till a
    long shadow fell on pedlars
and far away the sound of hoofs / increased in moonlight /
    whole cities crouched in saddlebags
churches, dungeons, juntas dangled from reins / like grasses
    picked from the rank fields
and drops of halter sweat
burned men to the bone, but the hare
like mad / played

Death in Duke Street

A huddle on the greasy street –
cars stop, nose past, withdraw –
dull glint on soles of tackety boots,
frayed rough blue trousers, nondescript coat
stretching back, head supported
in strangers' arms, a crowd collecting –
'Whit's wrang?' 'Can ye see'm?'

'An auld fella, he's had it.'
On one side, a young mother in a headscarf
is kneeling to comfort him, her three-year-old son
stands puzzled, touching her coat, her shopping-bag
spills its packages that people look at
as they look at everything. On the other side
a youth, nervous, awkwardly now
at the centre of attention as he shifts his arm
on the old man's shoulders, wondering
what to say to him, glancing up at the crowd.
These were next to him when he fell,
and must support him into death.
He seems not to be in pain,
he is speaking slowly and quietly
but he does not look at any of them,
his eyes are fixed on the sky,
already he is moving out
beyond everything belonging.
As if he still belonged
they hold him very tight.

Only the hungry ambulance
howls for him through the staring squares.

.

Stobhill

THE DOCTOR

Yes, I agreed to perform the abortion.
The girl was under unusual strain.
I formed the opinion that for personal reasons
and home circumstances her health would suffer
if pregnancy was not terminated.
She was unmarried and the father was unknown.
She had important exams to sit,
her career would be jeopardized, and in any case
she went in mortal fear of her father
(who is himself, as it happens, a doctor)

and believed he would throw her out of the house.
These factors left me in no doubt.
Accordingly I delivered her seven months baby
without complications. It was limp and motionless.
I was satisfied there was no life in it.
Normal practice was followed: it was placed
in a paper disposal bag and sent
to the incinerator. Later to my surprise
I was told it was alive. It was then returned
and I massaged its chest and kept it warm.
It moved and breathed about eight hours.
Could it have lived? I hardly think so.
You call it a disturbing case? Disturbing
is a more emotive word than I would choose
but I take the point. However, the child
as far as I was concerned was dead
on delivery, and my disposal instructions
were straight and without melodrama.
There is, as sheriff and jury will agree,
an irony for students of the human condition
(and in this case who is not?)
in the fact that the baby was resuscitated
by the jogging of the bag on its way to the incinerator.
I hope that everything I have said is clear.

THE BOILERMAN

Ay well, the porter brought this bag doon
(he'd come fae the operatin theatre like)
an he sayed it wis fur burnin.
Ah tellt him it would have tae wait,
ah had tae clean the fire oot first,
say hauf an oor, then it could go in.
So he goes away an leaves the bag,
it wis on a big pile of bags, like, all ready
fur tae go in. Anyway, ah gote the fire up,
ah starts throwin bags in the incinerator,
an ah'm luftin this wee bag an
ah hear a sorta whimperin – cryin like –
an ah can feel somethin breathin
through the paper. Whit did ah dae?
Ah pit it on a binch, near the hote pipes.

78

An ah goes up thae sterrs fur the porter.
Asks him, What wis in that bag?
He says, A foetus. Ah says, What's that?
A kiddy, he says. D'ye ken it's alive? ah says.
He says, Yes. Ah says, It's a bluidy shame,
is it no? He says, Ay it's a bluidy shame.
But the sleekit bugger never let dab
when he brought the bag. All he sayed wis burn it
and that's the God's truth. It's bad enough
whit the doctors dae, but he'd have been a murderer
if ah hadny heard the wean cryin –
Christ, it was hingin ower the fire –
may-be a quick death in thae degrees,
but ah couldny sleep fur nights
thinkin aboot it, couldny sleep
an och, ah still think what's the use,
ah didny save the kiddy's life.
It canny have been meant tae live.
An yet ye'd wonder, wid ye no?

THE MOTHER

I've no idea who the father is.
I took a summer job in a hotel
in the Highlands, there was a party, I
got drunk, it must have happened then
but I remember nothing. When I knew
I was pregnant I was almost crazy,
it seemed the end of everything.
My father – it was just impossible,
you have no idea what he is like,
he would certainly have turned me out
and made my mother's life unbearable
if it wasn't unbearable before.
If I can describe him, he is a man
who equates permissive with diabolical.
Reading about a drug-raid once at breakfast
he threw a chair across the room
and swore till he was purple – swearing's
all right, and malt whisky, and chair-breaking,
but not sex. I have sometimes wondered
how he got over conceiving me,

79

or perhaps – if he ever did get over it.
– I am sorry, this is irrelevant.
I wanted to say that I – my actions
are not very good and I don't defend them,
but I could not have the baby,
I just could not, you do see?
And now I never want to have one,
that's what it's done to me. I'm sick
of thinking, regretting, wishing, blaming.
I've gone so dead I see it all
like pulled from someone else's womb
and I can almost pity her
till I remember I'd be best
to forget the loss was mine.

THE FATHER
Did she? Did she? I'm really not surprised
I'm really not. Vodka, rum, gin –
some night yon was. Was it me?
Was it my bairn? Christ I don't know,
it might have been, I had her all right –
but there were three of us you know –
at least three – there was big Alec
and the wee French waiter wi the limp
(what d'ye cry him, Louie, wee Louie) –
and we went to this hut down by the loch –
it was a perfect night, perfect night –
mind you, we were all staggering a bit
but she was the worst let me tell you.
Big Alec, he's standing behind her and
kinna nibbling her neck and he leans over
and pulls her breasts out and says What have we here?
and she's giggling with her hair all over the place –
she looked that stupit we were all laughing, –
no, I'm telling a lie, we werny all laughing,
I'll aye remember the French kid, Louie,
he wasny laughing, eyes like wee ferrets
as if he'd never seen yon before, and maybe
he hadn't, but he couldny take his eyes off her.
We got in the hut, into the hut
and see her, soon as we were in that door –

80

out like a light, flat on her back.
Well, I got going, then the other two,
but if you ask me they didny do much,
they'd had a right skinful and they were –
anyhow, I don't remember much after that,
it all goes a bit hazy. But I do remember
coming out the hut it was a lovely night,
it was July and it was a lovely night
with the big trees and the water an all.

THE PORTER
Ah know ah tellt them lies at the enquiry.
Ah sayed ah thought the wean wis dead
when ah took it tae the incinerator.
Ah didny think the wean wis dead,
but ah didny ken fur shair, did ah?
It's no fur me tae question the doctors.
Ah get a bag fae the sister, right?
She says take that an burn it. She's only
passin on the doctor's instructions,
but she seen the wean, she thought it wis dead,
so ye canny blame her. And the doctor says
ye canny blame him. Everybody wants
tae come doon on me like a tonna bricks.
Ah canny go aboot openin disposal bags –
if ah did ah'd be a nervous wreck.
Ah passed two electricians in the corridor
an ah tellt them the wean wis alive
but they thought ah wis jokin. Efter that
ah jist shut up, an left it tae the boilerman
tae fin oot fur hissel – he couldny miss it
could he? The puir wee thing wis squeelin
through the bag wis it no? Ah canny see
ah had tae tell him whit was evident.
– Ah know ah'm goin on aboot this.
But suppose the kiddy could've been saved –
or suppose the boilerman hadny noticed it –
mah wee lassie's gote a hamster, ye ken? –
and ah fixed up a treadmill fur it
and it goes roon an roon an roon –
it's jist like that. Well ah'm no in court noo.

Don't answer nothing incriminatin, says the sheriff.
And that's good enough fur yours truly.
And neither ah did, neither ah did,
neither ah did, neither ah did.

Glasgow Sonnets

i

A mean wind wanders through the backcourt trash.
Hackles on puddles rise, old mattresses
puff briefly and subside. Play-fortresses
of brick and bric-a-brac spill out some ash.
Four storeys have no windows left to smash,
but in the fifth a chipped sill buttresses
mother and daughter the last mistresses
of that black block condemned to stand, not crash.
Around them the cracks deepen, the rats crawl.
The kettle whimpers on a crazy hob.
Roses of mould grow from ceiling to wall.
The man lies late since he has lost his job,
smokes on one elbow, letting his coughs fall
thinly into an air too poor to rob.

ii

A shilpit dog fucks grimly by the close.
Late shadows lengthen slowly, slogans fade.
The YY PARTICK TOI grins from its shade
like the last strains of some lost *libera nos
a malo*. No deliverer ever rose
from these stone tombs to get the hell they made
unmade. The same weans never make the grade.
The same grey street sends back the ball it throws.
Under the darkness of a twisted pram
a cat's eyes glitter. Glittering stars press
between the silent chimney-cowls and cram
the higher spaces with their SOS.
Don't shine a torch on the ragwoman's dram.
Coats keep the evil cold out less and less.

82

iii

'See a tenement due for demolition?
I can get ye rooms in it, two, okay?
Seven hundred and nothin legal to pay
for it's no legal, see? That's my proposition,
ye can take it or leave it but. The position
is simple, you want a hoose, I say
for eight hundred pound it's yours.' And they
trailing five bairns, accepted his omission
of the foul crumbling stairwell, windows wired
not glazed, the damp from the canal, the cooker
without pipes, packs of rats that never tired –
any more than the vandals bored with snooker
who stripped the neighbouring houses, howled, and fired
their aerosols – of squeaking 'Filthy lucre!'

iv

Down by the brickworks you get warm at least.
Surely soup-kitchens have gone out? It's not
the Thirties now. Hugh MacDiarmid forgot
in 'Glasgow 1960' that the feast
of reason and the flow of soul has ceased
to matter to the long unfinished plot
of heating frozen hands. We never got
an abstruse song that charmed the raging beast.
So you have nothing to lose but your chains,
dear Seventies. Dalmarnock, Maryhill,
Blackhill and Govan, better sticks and stanes
should break your banes, for poets' words are ill
to hurt ye. On the wrecker's ball the rains
of greeting cities drop and drink their fill.

v

'Let them eat cake' made no bones about it.
But we say let them eat the hope deferred
and that will sicken them. We have preferred
silent slipways to the riveters' wit.
And don't deny it – that's the ugly bit.
Ministers' tears might well have launched a herd
of bucking tankers if they'd been transferred
from Whitehall to the Clyde. And smiles don't fit
either. 'There'll be no bevvying' said Reid
at the work-in. But all the dignity you muster
can only give you back a mouth to feed
and rent to pay if what you lose in bluster
is no more than win patience with 'I need'
while distant blackboards use you as their duster.

vi

The North Sea oil-strike tilts east Scotland up,
and the great sick Clyde shivers in its bed.
But elegists can't hang themselves on fled-
from trees or poison a recycled cup –
If only a less faint, shaky sunup
glimmered through the skeletal shop and shed
and men washed round the piers like gold and spread
golder in soul than Mitsubishi or Krupp –
The images are ageless but the thing
is now. Without my images the men
ration their cigarettes, their children cling
to broken toys, their women wonder when
the doors will bang on laughter and a wing
over the firth be simply joy again.

Environmentalists, ecologists
and conservationists are fine no doubt.
Pedestrianization will come out
fighting, riverside walks march off the lists,
pigeons and starlings be somnambulists
in far-off suburbs, the sandblaster's grout
multiply pink piebald façades to pout
at sticky-fingered mock-Venetianists.
Prop up's the motto. Splint the dying age.
Never displease the watchers from the grave.
Great when fake architecture was the rage,
but greater still to see what you can save.
The gutted double fake meets the adage:
a wig's the thing to beat both beard and shave.

Meanwhile the flyovers breed loops of light
in curves that would have ravished tragic Toshy –
clean and unpompous, nothing wishy-washy.
Vistas swim out from the bulldozer's bite
by day, and banks of earthbound stars at night
begin. In Madame Emé's Sauchie Haugh, she
could never gain in leaves or larks or sploshy
lanes what's lost in a dead boarded site –
the life that overspill is overkill to.
Less is not more, and garden cities are
the flimsiest oxymoron to distil to.
And who wanted to distil? Let bus and car
and hurrying umbrellas keep their skill to
feed ukiyo-e beyond Lochnagar.

ix

It groans and shakes, contracts and grows again.
Its giant broken shoulders shrug off rain.
It digs its pits to a shauchling refrain.
Roadworks and graveyards like their gallus men.
It fattens fires and murders in a pen
and lets them out in flaps and squalls of pain.
It sometimes tears its smoky counterpane
to hoist a bleary fist at nothing, then
at everything, you never know. The west
could still be laid with no one's tears like dust
and barricaded windows be the best
to see from till the shops, the ships, the trust
return like thunder. Give the Clyde the rest.
Man and the sea make cities as they must.

x

From thirtieth floor windows at Red Road
he can see choughs and samphires, dreadful trade –
the schoolboy reading *Lear* has that scene made.
A multi is a sonnet stretched to ode
and some say that's no joke. The gentle load
of souls in clouds, vertiginously stayed
above the windy courts, is probed and weighed.
Each monolith stands patient, ah'd and oh'd.
And stalled lifts generating high-rise blues
can be set loose. But stalled lives never budge.
They linger in the single-ends that use
their spirit to the bone, and when they trudge
from closemouth to laundrette their steady shoes
carry a world that weighs us like a judge.

Memories of Earth

They told me that the night and day were all that I could see;
They told me that I had five senses to enclose me up,
And they enclosed my infinite brain into a narrow circle
And sunk my heart into the abyss, a red round globe hot-burning,
till all from life I was obliterated and erased.

— Blake

My fingers tremble when I touch the tapes.
Since we came back from earth, nothing's the same.
I tell you I hear that sea beyond the glass
throwing its useless music away in handfuls.
Once I angled a sweet chair to catch it.
I never even walk there now, far less
imagine vacant nature has a song.
Yet it's not vacant, wasn't that the point?
I must avoid questions, exclamations.
Keep your report formal, said the Council,
your evidence is for the memory-banks,
not for crude wonder or cruder appraisal.
I only report that nature is not the same.
And I report it within the spirit
of our resolve, which is indeed our duty,
to record whatever we have found to be,
to meditate on everything recorded,
and to record our meditations till
the plain figure of promised order appears.
I served, I took the oath: but my hand shakes
as I take up the damaged tapes and play them.

TAPE 1: THE STONE

          . . . had to go to the north shore
of the inland sea. There are six of us.
The stone we are to enter is well marked,
lies in a hollow and is as big as my fist.
Indeed the temptation to cup it, lift it, throw it
is strong. We resist. Whatever signal it gives
or is thought to give, only just not too faint
to rouse the interest of central monitors,
to us it's silent, like the stone it is.

87

The shrinking must be done by stages, but
even so it comes with a rush, doesn't
feel like shrinking. Rather it's the landscape
explodes upwards, outwards, the waves rise up
and loom like waterfalls, and where we stand
our stone blots out the light above us, a crag
pitted with caves and tunnels, immovable
yet somehow less solid. We climb, squeeze in
and one by one tramp through the galleries
till we have reached the designated cavern,
fan out on the dim rubbly floor, and wait.
We shrink again – accelerated this time.
The rubble's a mountain-range, the shallow roof
a dark night sky in infinite soft distance.
The gallery we came by's like a black
hole in space. Off we go across the plain
into the new foothills. Have we moved at all?
I am not to speculate, only to explore
as commanded. I record it is harder now
to remember where we are, environment
tie-dyes memory into struggling patterns.
We always knew it stood to reason that
the smallest thing, seen close, would have some roughness,
but we could not envisage the sheer presence
of the blow-up, establishing its new world
each time, here, here, here; forget *there*, it says.
Dead though, all round, like a desert, and silent.
A desert in the middle of a stone!
– Erase the exclamation mark. Surprise
comes from old microstructure thinking.
We must stop that. We are beginning to learn
that where you are is what is, not less than
what is. 'You'd better not insult the Council,'
says Hlad. 'We're at the next diminishing-point.'
We sit together on the rocky slab,
join hands for safety, since the operation
must now be very fine, and suddenly
the six of us feel the whole desert-floor
strain outwards like a skin and burst in grains
of pale grey sand as large as asteroids.
We float to one, clamber aboard, and drift.
Space is like hard pure night traversed with flashes.

We must be near the atomic sub-structure.
I get a tenseness, Hazmon says vibration,
to Baltaz, with her keen ear, it seems music.
Kort stares at us, finds nothing, but 'Colder?'
he asks. My headache comes a little later.
But these are all expected signs; the Council
warned us the signals we are here to trace
(if they are signals) must be sending power
into a huge periphery, as our next stage
will tell. We brace ourselves for the last trip.
The asteroids boil up, swim out of sight,
we're plucked off into space by the force field
as cosmic dust and comets and star systems
grow out of nothing point by point of fire.
Our senders are directioning us now,
in slow shrinkdown, into a galaxy
that's soon wrapped round us with its long bright wings
and then expands as we contract until
it's tenuous and fair as haze. We're bound
for a smallish sort of sun, and planets
mushrooming about it, we don't move
but in our moving matrix we approach
the size that puts us in that system, lets
a too large world with rings go thundering past,
swells a speck of blue swirling with white
to a globe where millions of us could live,
white clouds and blue sky mount through us into
a strange protective canopy, and ground
of some sort rushes up to meet our feet
and scatters red and brown to far horizons
now the horizons of our sight. I'd say
the emanations here are like a source
of power; we've reached where we were sent; the new
blots out the old more strongly than before –
brown moor and yellow broom, a swooping bird
that clatters off some rocks with a wild cry,
and up there all those moving clouds, not fixed
as ours are in a chosen set but free
to drift and break as if they were not dead,
above a moorland where birds come and go
unchecked, wind shakes the easy heather bells
this way and that. In a dream we stand,

uncertain, abstracted, on the springy turf,
till 'Is there no Council here then?' asks Hlad,
and kills the spell. We tune in our receptors
but cannot unscramble the pervasive resonance.
Is it noise, and therefore not to be unscrambled,
or is it a simultaneity of signals,
or has their Council (if they have one) coded
their power for only equal power to crack?
Our expert, Tromro, gets to work on this.
Part of an unexpected answer comes,
not from Tromro, but from the landscape – it melts
at the edges like a photograph in flames,
throbs, re-forms, faces appear, a flare
of light on metal, swords ringing, a gold torque
filled with blood, the high whinny of horses,
dissolving back into a thrust of darkness.
It recomposes as a dusty plain
under a cloudless sky; we kick up dust;
we know now what we might have guessed: our time
and this world's time can never be in phase,
its images, its messages, its life
must come to us like an eternal present,
and by our very meagrest interfering
we trigger fragments of the vanished prints
but have no key to make the sequence clear.
Tromro will have to . . .

TAPE 2: THE EARTH

                    . . . so confused.
Questions come thick and fast, we don't erase them.
This is most dangerous. The Council warned
any questioning was theirs alone.
What makes us disobey them? There – again!
A question and an exclamation, both.
Are we disintegrating, are we growing?
We've grown so small we can perhaps re-enter
places only the bewildered can be great in,
as we've heard books and tapes say were once ours,
histories back, in the red days of action.
Even to think of those days is a reproach.

I know that but I do not feel it. So?
So we are all able to change, nothing
can quite put down susceptibility,
not that I claim it as a virtue when
it stirs like wearing thorns: I record this,
with what relevance none of us can say.
And what I must record I must record:
the wind shrieks now across a desolation
of mirages, splintered castles, reed-beds,
a stork forms fishing, horsemen heavily
come together, canter with whips in fog,
a sullen mob, restrained, an open space
and though the picture never quite comes clear
we see the bellows at the huge fire, then
tongs drag out a red-hot iron throne,
a peasant's forced to sit on it, his head
pressed into a red-hot crown, his hand
clasped round a red-hot sceptre while the smoke
swirls over jeering breath: long live the king!
long live King Dózsa! and the rearing horses
foam at their jerked bits like an old frieze
till suddenly the whole scene snaps tight shut
and we're left staring at a sea of clouds.
We must be on some mountain-top at night,
with a full moon riding the black above
but tongues and limbs of mist stretching below,
mist or cloud we can hardly be sure,
cloud or sea we can hardly be sure
as the white masses die in distant grey
and hills might be the whales they loom like there,
but we imagine waves all round us, ride
on our mountain as moons ride their dark air.
We watch three climbers; a dog sniffs the rock;
one gaunt man stands apart, brooding intently
over the metamorphosis, we think
it's what he says we hear through the vague roar
of what must be big unseen mountain-streams.
'The emblem of a mind that feeds upon
infinity, that broods over the dark abyss,
intent to hear its voices issuing forth
to silent light in one continuous stream.'
The dog barks, and the scene strains out in white.

Facing us is a gigantic screen.
Scores of steamed-up cars are parked in rows.
A couple locked or twisting in a kiss
is silhouetted smoochily in each.
The summer desert air has stars, the screen
that no one looks at flickers crazily
and howls distorted sound at love-bites. It's
only a painted cat up there, grinning
as it rolls a bulldog in a hammock and
batters it, thinking it's a mouse. The film,
the sand, the erotic jalopies, fade
in a slow dim-out towards Arizona.
A bleached signpost like a cactus revolves
as the earth turns. Flashes, stripes of darkness
clatter up like jarring shutters; landscapes
come and go, at last one slows down, holds,
shimmering in a fine red autumn haze.
It seems a camp in time of war – barbed wire,
watchtowers, rows of huts, but also blocks
(too many surely to be bakeries)
with huge square chimneys – acrid smoke from one
drifts off over the stubble-fields. A train
of cattle-trucks has brought in new arrivals,
two thousand perhaps, men, women, children,
all ages, tired or apprehensive, joking,
reassuring, glad to stretch their legs,
filing into a hall with hooks for clothes.
A sign says BATH AND DISINFECTION ROOM.
Guards tell them to undress, help the worried,
the old, the sick; mothers help their children,
hush their crying; young couples hand in hand
smile at their nakedness, but some men sweat,
half-hide their fear, one moans, shakes like litmus.
In ten minutes all are ready, the guards
herd them to the farther door, unscrewing
the strange wheel that is its handle, and
all troop into the disinfection room,
some driven struggling, the last few screaming
as the thick oak door is screwed smoothly shut.
The beating on the panels mounts, and dies,
a thin susurrus filters through a while
like what I've read of spirits suffering,

but nothing is in my understanding.
I stare at Baltaz, who has clung to me
as if she was a woman of the earth,
and nothing on her features is not pain.
We have no pain, we cannot suffer pain.
I have nothing I can say to her but
'I saw no bath or cloth or soap or tap.
There was nothing but cement walls and floor,
and perforated columns of sheet-iron.
How do we know what earthmen do?' 'I know!'
she cries, 'I know what they do! Record it!
They make people into ash, turn babies
into smoke. Is that the message they've sent
out over all their puny universe?
Is that what scratched at our dish? The Council
sends explorers for a handful of that?
Dust, bones, gold rings, old women's rags? Take me
out of this earth, Erlkon, take us away.'
Before I can answer her, thunderclaps
bang sheets of rain across the fields, the camp
wavers, blotted out, is gone. We're left with
a heather moor like one we saw before,
and now it's hot: bees hum; the panic goes.
A butterfly's an epaulette on Kort's
thin shoulder, Hazmon laughs, holds out a twig
and the white creature flutters to it, Hlad
thinks this is childish but even he's benign.
Only Baltaz looks at the butterfly
as if she would cup its frailty for ever
against the eerie furnaces. She's changed.
I'm changing. I record this without comment.
For I don't want us recalled yet, not yet.
We must expose ourselves to it. To what? To that.
The Council will note I conserve questions.
Tromro has banks of information, Kort
spores, Hazmon has his films, Hlad and I the tapes,
Baltaz – Baltaz –
                          Sunset, in what I've read
is beauty, even glory, crowns the earth
with harmless fires. Colours of great fineness
from pearl to crimson to dark purple coast
and flush and doze and deepen and decay

in shapes we'd never give a name to in
a hundred days of watching them dissolve.
And now the stars come out above the hill.
It seems this is a world of change, where we,
observing, can scarcely fix the observed
and are unfixed ourselves. This solid hill
even as I speak is half transparent,
white walls and floors show through, we sink, the stars
are roof-lights in a large computer room.
The air is clear, the light even, the hall
vibrant as a heart. A screen we approach
switches itself on, flickers, fills with snow,
focuses to a powerful image
grainy and stark in grey-green, black and white.
Figures in domes – men, women – work and move.
They've left the earth, like seeds. Is it their moon,
or a near planet, or have they gone out
beyond their system into some neighbour
millimetre in the stone? – Tromro's job.
But now with an extreme concerted movement
the milling hundreds in one dome turn round
to face us, and the screen is scored with gestures
that make us catch our breath as they stretch out
arms seeming to implore us where we stand.
And every face flickers with white longing,
and some on knees, or drooping propped on friends,
or sunk with hair that sweeps the floor, some straight
and motionless in such a dignity,
some streaked with crying, all in such a case
we can but take as last or next to last
in desperation, and the time unknown
past, future, or the myriad-to-one
unthinkable and terrible present.
If it is now, we cannot save them; past,
what we feel must surely be pain; to come,
it's like a warning of all fate we've read
waits, though we must not believe it. The screen
scrambles in points of bluish light, goes blank.
We sit at consoles that go ghostly as
we search the data banks. Fragments of sound
clash out and shred to silence – *seventeen* –
leaning – a prominence – Christ yes man go –

solitaire et glacé – shoot from – eagles –
vstayot zarya vo mglye kholodnoy – burn –
done with Danny Deever – programme – Sturm und –
a gabble in a wilderness of wires,
an earth labouring in memories.
And soon we're in a void of echoes, faint
and more faint, merging with a rising wind
that stirs the greatest of the earth's huge seas.
It is all round us, boundless to the eye
although we know it is not boundless, blue
and blue-grey, steely, warmer green, green-black
with flecks of whipped-up white and longish swells
where hints of prussian browns, acid yellows,
glass pinks that only numbered charts could name
crosshatch the windy sharkskin; real sharkskin's
not far under, and tumbling whales; typhoon's
kingdom too. But now only a handful
of clouds is scattered through the morning sky.
The sun begins to walk on the Pacific.
And now we see and come down closer to
a speck that does not fit that emptiness.
A thousand miles from land, this black canoe,
long, broad, and strongly built, with fine high prow
much ornamented, and many oars, drives
forward steady across the zigzag sun-prints.
Tattoos as intricate as the prow-carving
stand out on the brown arms and backs and brows
as men who might be warriors bend and row,
yet seem explorers and not war-men, for their boat
has stores for major voyaging, animals,
children, and women slicing coconuts
and shaking back their long black shining hair,
offering rowers the fresh smiling milk.
The men are singing as they row, the chant
comes up, torn off in buffets of the wind,
returns in strength. By the gunwale a cock crows.
Whatever far-off landfall is their goal,
known or unknown, or only hoped-for, they
have crossed dangerous immensity
like a field, and dangerous immensity
to come lies all about them without land:
their life is with the waves and wind, they move

95

forward in ordinary fortitude,
and someday they'll steer through that Southern Cross
they only steer by now.
                         There's a loud hum,
and swirling shadows fill the air. Hlad warns
he feels the signs are we must go. Tromro,
listening, confirms. It comes swifter than a blow.
The earth shrinks to a smaller point in space
than even the canoe was in its ocean.
A nebula like a riddle of flour
tempts us to shake out a few million worlds
in passing; fate might bake a thing from that.
Remagnification euphoria
is fiercer than we'd thought. We keep control
and wait for the next phase to . . .

END OF TAPE 2

I think not much was missing from that tape.
The phases came in order, without crisis.
We crept out of the rock, shot up, looked back
at what was now a stone again, ourselves
in our old scale of body, dune, and sea.
How uninteresting those dunes, that sea!
We made our report in a troubled confusion,
memories flashing between sentences
to make us falter, stare at the Council
as if they were an alien life-form. Hopeless –
they soon gave up politeness, froze us, said
our report was totally deplored, useless
to contemplate, ruinously incomplete;
feeling and action had besotted us;
our anti-brainwashing sessions had been
a clinic wasted; was earth such a paragon
or paradise or paradigm that we
lost our nature in a simple phasing? –
and they'd be training non-susceptibles
for a further expedition. What I suspect
is that susceptibility's a pearl of price,
now that I've heard the tapes again. It's true
the mission failed: we don't know whether earth
is sending or had sent a message or

was itself the message in dying it became,
though this too might be a real message sent
by the survivors gone to other stars.
We don't know even if there are survivors
now, for when is now? To me it seems
the virtue's in the questions, not the answers.
I think this fishbone's in the Council's throat,
for all their smoothing of the rule-book. It was
infinity the poet on the mountain said
the mind must feed on, which is very fine,
and I agree with it, but when we reach
the almost infinitely small and find
well-made extermination camps, nothing
seems infinite except cruelty, nothing
feeds the mind but processions to death.
Not true, not true. What is that infinite hope
that forces a canoe upon the waters,
infinite love in the woman comforting
her child at the mortal bathhouse door?
I think the break came when we showed the film
of Dózsa sizzling on his throne. 'Cut,' said
Council. 'We're not impressed by drops of sweat.
A xerox of the execution order
would suffice. Couldn't you see the man's been dead
this thousand thousand years?' 'No, he's not dead,'
I said. The Council stared as if I was
an alien life-form, which perhaps I am
now. How do I know whether Dózsa's dead?
Why don't the dead just disappear then? What
if the Council are all hallucinants
projected by hostile powers to keep us mild?
Who told who to tell us not to feel?
tell us love's wrong, leads to suffering?
hate's wrong, leads to fire and battlefields?
and questions above all are wrong, lead to
deflected meditation on the order
we wait to see: who says? What use is order
to a chained world under a painted sky?
If any order's there we'd break it like
a shell to let some living touch emerge.
Frail, frail, frail! Better than those pavilions
of molybdenum, demagnification banks

that rev for our successors! The cock crows still,
I hear it, praise it, on that southern sea.
The voyagers are out, the day is up,
and that's what we record at last.

                              We meet
in secret now, the six of us, from time
to time, and study how to change this life.
Baltaz has moved in with me; everything
seems like a great wave shining disclosed
travelling our planet's deadwater. Tromro
has taught us much; each frame of Hazmon's film
is burned into our minds; Hlad's tapes have noise
– every sound on earth – and mine have voice.
Baltaz is at her handbook: what we must do,
and when. But uncommunicative Kort's
our *wunderkind* (as earthmen say), he's made
a culture of the spores, they're growing at
their work not just of telling us what they are
but handing to our memories of earth
a life we'll make a source of life, begun
in purposes of rebuked pain and joy.

The World

1

I don't think it's not going onward,
though no one said it was a greyhound.
I don't accept we're wearing late.

I don't see the nothing some say anything
that's not in order comes to be found.
It may be nothing to be armour-plated.

I don't believe that what's been made
clutters the spirit. Let it be patented
and roll. It never terrorized

three ikon angels sitting at a table
in Moscow, luminous as a hologram
and blessing everything from holograms

to pliers at a dripping nail.
I don't believe it's not the wrench
of iron that let the body fall.

2

There was this unholy scuffle.
They felled the sober with the tipsy.
At last someone got pushed mildly

onto a breadknife. As he observed
in the ward, What's more, what's more,
just nobody's going to go there.

They did though. Even if which was which
was always a guessing-game, the case
meant the whole scene had bristles on.

Expressionless hardmen glittered. Sleepwalkers
jived. There was a dog. Before
the end of the evening a desire

for everything had returned, very
smoky it's true, but true. The sleeper
in the ward was the only one with nightmares.

3

Sometimes it swells like the echo of a passion
dying with paeans, not sighs. Who
knows the weight and list of its rebellions?

Underneath, underneath, underneath, underneath –
you think it beats in the age-old fashion,
even red, perhaps, like a pre-set strawberry

creeping below the crust? It's artistic
to have ordered impulses. To
think the world has makes you feel great.

Beyond the world, the slow-dying sun
flares out a signal fan, projecting
a million-mile arm in skinny hydrogen

to flutter it at our annals.
Coarse, knee-deep in years, we
go on counting, miss the vast unreason.

4

Technologies like dragonflies, the strange
to meet the strange; and at the heart
of things, who knows what is dependent?

Imagine anything the world could, it might
do; anything not to do, it would.
A plume of act flies as it spins by.

We saw the nettles in the ancient station.
The signalbox was like a windmill, haunted
by bats and autumn wasps. She

twirled a scarf through leaves. Remembrance
offered nothing, swam in our hands.
We're here. The past is not our home.

I don't think it's not being perfect
that brings the sorrows in, but being soon
beyond the force not to be powerless.

Shaker Shaken

Ah pe-an t-as ke t-an te loo
O ne vas ke than sa-na was-ke
    lon ah ve shan too
Te wan-se ar ke ta-ne voo te
    lan se o-ne voo
Te on-e wan tase va ne woo te wan-se o-ne van
Me-le wan se oo ar ke-le van te
    shom-ber on vas sa la too lar var sa
    re-voo an don der on v-tar loo-cum an la voo
O be me-sum ton ton ton tol-a wac-er tol-a wac-er
    ton ton te s-er pane love ten poo

Ah pe-an t-as ke t-an tiger
O ne vas ke than tuft of was-ke
    lon ah ve shan tree
Te wan-se ar ke ta-ne voodoo
    lan se opal voo
Te on-e-wan likely va ne woo te wan-se o-ne stonework
Me-le white se oo ar ke-le van off
    shom-ber blown over sa la too lar var sa
    following an don der on opal loo-cum an la voo
O be me-sum ton ton mixed with a wac-er tol-a wac-er
    ton ton tiger pane love ten poo

That pe-an t-as saw t-an tiger
O ne vas through a tuft of was-ke
    by the ve shan tree
Nothing ar ke ta-ne voodoo
    till se opal voo
Nothing on-e-wan likely to ne woo te wan-se o-ne stonework
till a white se oo ar ke-le us off
    shom-ber blown over the la too without harm
    following an don der on opal losing our voo
O be me-sum ton ton mixed with the waters the tol-a wac-er
    ton ton tiger swam with us loved ten poo

That was when t-as saw the tiger
O ne vas through a tuft of morning-glory
    by the ve scraped tree
Nothing in the air ta-ne voodoo

till the opal voo
Nothing seemed likely to ne woo te wan-se old stonework
till a white lot of ar ke-le us off
    shom-ber blown over the lake without harm
    following flakes on opal losing our tracks
O be me-sum and we mixed with the waters the wily waters
    till the tiger swam with us loved ten poo

That was when we saw the tiger
yawning through a tuft of morning-glory
    by the well-scraped tree
Nothing in the air suggested voodoo
    till the opal fell
Nothing seemed likely to go warmer than old stonework
till a white lot of flame took us off
    suddenly blown over the lake without harm
    following flakes of opal losing our tracks
in tiger's-eyes and we mixed with the waters the wily waters
    till the tiger swam with us and loved us up

[The first stanza is a Shaker sound-poem of 1847.]

Vico's Song

    the universe that turned in on itself
    turned in on itself
    on itself
    self was
    was the universe
    that was turned in
    it was the universe that was turned in

    the universe that was turned in
    turned in got seven
    seven days
    days it
    it spent turning
    spent turning over
    days it spent turning over a new leaf

the universe that turned over a new leaf
turned over a new leaf
new leaf
leaf lived
lived in the arms
in the arms of the eternal
it lived in the arms of the eternal return

Resurrections

None of your jade suits, none of your gold-sewn princes! –
green-shelled spoonfuls of dust like coelacanths in tombs.
I want to be born again. Keep Tollund peat
for roses, boots, blazes. Men of Han, princesses,
yellowing demons and mummies, casket-crowders,
haunt off! There's never armour made
I'd pray to be preserved in. Don't preserve me!
Yesterday great Chou's ashes flew
in the wind over plain and river,
never resting or rusting, nothing
for an urn. Unknown he blows
like seed, is seed,
a little cinnamon of the millennium.
Let them roll away the black diorite
where millions shuffle past a husk.
What? Christ too like Chou could not be found.
In this strange January spring,
so mild the blackbirds go mad
singing in the morning above Anniesland,
I woke, I heard them, no one at my side,
but thought of you with the exhilaration
of that rising song where like them I scatter
and swoop in rings over the half-dark earth,
caught up in another life.

Particle Poems

1
The old old old old particle
smiled. 'I grant you I'm not beautiful,'
he said, 'but I've got charm.
It's charm that's led me where I am.'

Opened up his bosom, showed me a quark.
It gleamed. He grinned like a clam. 'Sort
of heart, really, though I've got four.
They're in orbit, and what for

is a good question, unless to pump up
charm. I know I must look a frump
– just fishing – but seriously
would you not say I'm easily

the nearest thing to doom and centrehood
you've ever been unable to preclude?
Cathedrals – oh, antiquities and slime,
knucklebones, teeth five feet long, signs

and wonders, auks, knuckledusters,
twangs from armchairs, waters
waiting to break, cells waiting to squeak,
a sniff of freesia, a book

of hours, and hours themselves like days
in love, and even nanoseconds raised
by charm to higher powers, wait
until I make them, and fade.'

Shot off – never showed his age.

2
The young particle screamed round the bend,
braked hard, broke.
His mother dozing in Manchuria
heard his last cry. A mare's ear twitched.
Dust, and dust, the wires sang.

104

3

Three particles lived in mystical union.
They made knife, fork, and spoon,
and earth, sea, and sky.
They made animal, vegetable, and mineral,
and faith, hope, and charity.
They made stop, caution, go,
and hickory, dickory, dock.
They made yolk, white, and shell,
and hook, line, and sinker.
They made pounds, shillings, and pence,
and Goneril, Regan, and Cordelia.
They made Shadrach, Meshach, and Abednego,
and game, set, and match.

A wandering particle kidnapped one of them,
and the two that were left made day and night,
and left and right, and right and wrong,
and black and white, and off and on,
but things were never quite the same,
and two will always yearn for three.
They're after you, or me.

4

Part particle and part idea, she
struggled through a throb of something.
A wheatear, or an ear of wheat?
How could she possibly know
beyond the shrill vibrations, sunny fibres, field?
What was the field but forces, surges?
To veins of green and veins of red
she was colour-blind. Well, she was blind.
But was she there at all –
when the wind ruffled that nest of growing things
and it took its course in the sun?

5

The particle that decided
got off its mark, but died.

6

Their mausoleum
is a frozen silent flak.
The fractured tracks,
photographed, docket
dead dogfights,
bursts of no malice.
Almost pure direction
points its stream,
deflected, detected.
Better than ogam
or cuneiform the tracer
of telling particles
fans out angrily
itself, itself, itself –
who we were
were here, here,
we died at the crossroads
or we defected
or we raced ahead
to be burnt out.
Faint paths hardly score,
yet shake the lens, end
in lucider mosaics
of theory. Go,
bid the soldiers shoot.

A Home in Space

Laid-back in orbit, they found their minds.
They found their minds were very clean and clear.
Clear crystals in swarms outside were their fireflies and larks.
Larks they were in lift-off, swallows in soaring.
Soaring metal is flight and nest together.
Together they must hatch.
Hatches let the welders out.
Out went the whitesuit riggers with frames as light as air.

Air was millions under lock and key.
Key-ins had computers wild on Saturday nights.
Nights, days, months, years they lived in space.
Space shone black in their eyes.
Eyes, hands, food-tubes, screens, lenses, keys were one.
One night – or day – or month – or year – they all –
all gathered at the panel and agreed –
agreed to cut communication with –
with the earth base – and it must be said they were –
were cool and clear as they dismantled the station and –
and gave their capsule such power that –
that they launched themselves outwards –
outwards in an impeccable trajectory, that band –
that band of tranquil defiers, not to plant any –
any home with roots but to keep a –
a voyaging generation voyaging, and as far –
as far as there would ever be a home in space –
space that needs time and time that needs life.

The Mouth .

I saw a great mouth in space that fifty thousand angels could not fill
they ran shrieking from it as it grew and threw their coloured coats
     and flares
for lures among the stars while it advanced and swallowed the
     planets of the sun
one by one and then the sun

it rose and swayed the Milky Way collapsed into it like a poorly
     shuffled pack
deeper and deeper into darkness it brought darkness and what it
     blotted out
it grew drunk on to grinning-point with so much fire in its belly it
     roared
over its thankless hoard

for that was the new horror to hear it when it howled like a hungry
    scraped womb
and galaxies jampacked with glittering rayed-out million-year-old
    civilizations
were jumped like a handful of asteroids and sucked into tales of hell
for all they could tell

the Plough long gone the winding Dragon the Lyre the Balance the
    fading Charioteer
Aquarius with a loud cry Keel Stern and Sails in terrible rushing
    silence
and now white Sirius was black yellow Capella was black red
    Antares was black
and no lights ever came back

heavens and paradises popped like seaweed eternal laws were
    never seen again
angels' teeth were cosmic dust and cosmic dust was angels' teeth
    all's grist
to that dark mill where christs and godbearers were pulped with
    their domes ikons vanes
their scrolls aeons and reigns

in Virgo the most evolved life there was was calm and watchful in
    its fiery coverts
the mouth had long been computed probable and plans had been
    laid and re-laid
the dense cluster of three thousand galaxies had made itself a force
    field
that would not know how to yield

the worlds of Virgo were not only inhabited but hyperinhabited
    they were all
one life and their force field was themselves they were a wall they
    shone they stood
jehovahs and elohim are daguerreotypes to their movies they
    made universes
as poets make verses

in Virgo they did not underestimate the mouth they were the last
    star-gate and goal
when they saw there were no other lights in the recesses of space
    and it was hard
to distinguish the shadow of the unsated mouth from the shadow
    of the dead
but its lips were blackest red

they gaped for Virgo with a scream they gaped for Virgo with a
scream they gaped for Virgo with a scream they gaped for Virgo
with a scream they gaped for Virgo with a scream they gaped
at that great quiet gate

The Moons of Jupiter

AMALTHEA

I took a book with me to Amalthea
but never turned a page. It weighed like lead.
I squatted with it like a grey image
malleted into the rock, listlessly
reading, staring, rereading listlessly
sentences that never came to anything.
My very memory lay paralysed
with everything else on that bent moon,
pulled down and dustbound, flattened, petrified
by gravitation, sweeping Jupiter's
more than half the sky with sentences
half-formed that never came to anything.
My tongue lay like a coil of iron, the planet
never heard a word. What did I say there?
My very memory is paralysed.
The book has gone too – I know how it began
but that first sentence never came to anything.
'The local train, with its three coaches, pulled up
at Newleigh Station at half-past four . . .'
The tons of pages never moved, my knees
were tombs, and though slow Jupiter slid past,

my memory of it is paralysed.
The stupid moon goes round. The local train,
with its three coaches pulled up at Newleigh Station
at half-past four, never comes to anything.
They rescued me with magnets, plucked me up
like dislocated yards of groaning mandrake.
The satellite engulfed the book in dust.

IO

The sulphur mines on Io were on strike
when we arrived. I can't say I'm surprised.
Seventy-five men had just been killed
in the fiercest eruption ever seen there.
I hardly recognized the grim volcano
with its rakish new centre and a leaning plume
two hundred miles high – like an ash tree,
someone said. Meanwhile the landscape burned,
not that it never burned before, but this
was roaring, sheeted, cruel. Empty
though not perfunctory funeral rites
had been performed; not a body was found.
The weird planetman's flute from friends in grief –
my god what a strange art it is, rising
so many million miles from home into
the raw thin cindery air – was the first sound
we heard when we stepped from the ship. We saw
the men huddled in knots, or walking slowly
with bent heads over the pumice beds, or still
and silent by the bank of the red lake.
The laser probes, the belts, the brilliant console
sat dark and motionless, crawled through by smoke.
Sulphur blew to choke the very soul.
We prospected beyond the lava-fields,
but the best sulphur's the most perilous.
The planetman must shoulder sorrow, great sacks
of pain, in places with no solace but
his own and what the winds and days may bring.

EUROPA

Boots and boats – in our bright orange gear
we were such an old-fashioned earthly lot
it seemed almost out of time-phase. We learned
or re-learned how to skate and ski, use snowshoes,
fish through ice-holes though not for fish. Soundings
and samples were our prey. We'd never grade
in years, far less in weeks, the infinite
play and glitter of watery Europa,
waters of crust ice, waters of deep ice,
waters of slush, of warm subcrustal springs,
waters of vapour, waters of water.
One day, and only one, we drilled right down
to something solid and so solid-hard
the drill-head screamed into the microphone
and broke, the film showed streaks of metal shards
whizzing across a band of basalt or
glimmery antediluvian turtle-shell
or cast-off titan miner's helmet or –
it must have been the metal scream that roused
our thought and fear and half desire we might
have had a living scream returned. Lightly
it sleeps, the imagination. On that smooth moon
men would be driven mad with many dreams,
hissing along the hill-less shining wastes,
or hearing the boat's engine chug the dark
apart, as if a curtain could be drawn
to let the living see even the dead
if they had once had life, if not that life.

GANYMEDE

Galileo would have been proud of Ganymede.
Who can call that marbled beauty dead?
Dark basins sweeping to a furrowed landfall,
gigantic bright-rayed craters, vestiges
and veils of ice and snow, black swirling grey,
grey veined with green, greens diffused in blues,
blue powdered into white: a king marble
rolled out, and set in place, from place to place.
We never landed, only photographed

111

and sent down probes from orbit; turbulence
on Jupiter was extreme, there was no lingering.
Is it beauty, or minerals, or knowledge
we take our expeditions for? What a question!
But is it What a question? Is it excitement,
or power, or understanding, or illumination
we take our expeditions for? Is it specimens,
or experiments, or spin-off, or fame, or evolution,
or necessity we take our expeditions for?
We are here, and our sons or our sons' sons
will be on Jupiter, and their sons' sons
at the star gate, leaving the fold of the sun.
I remember I drowsed off, dropped my notes,
with the image of Ganymede dancing before me.
They nudged me, smiling, said it was a judgement
for my wandering thoughts, what had got into me?
That satellite had iron and uranium.
We would be back. Well, that must be fine,
I teased them; had it gold, and asphodel?

CALLISTO

Scarred, cauterized, pocked and warty face:
you grin and gape and gawk and cock an ear
at us with craters, all blind, all deaf, all dumb,
toadback moon, brindled, brown and cold,
we plodded dryshod on your elephant-hide seas
and trundled gear from groove to groove, playing
the record of your past, imagining
the gross vales filled with unbombarded homes
they never had till we pitched nylon tents there:
radiation falling by the ton,
but days of meteorites long gone. Scatter
the yellow awnings, amaze the dust and ochre!
Frail and tough as flags we furnish out
the desolation. Even the greatest crater,
gouged as if a continent had struck it,
circled by rim on rim of ridges rippling
hundreds of miles over that slaty chaos,
cannot forbid our feet, our search, our songs.
I did not sing; the grave-like mounds and pits

112

reminded me of one grave long ago
on earth, when a high Lanarkshire wind
whipped out the tears men might be loath to show,
as if the autumn had a mercy I
could not give to myself, listening in shame
to the perfunctory priest and to my thoughts
that left us parted on a quarrel. These
memories, and love, go with the planetman
in duty and in hope from moon to moon.

The Mummy

(*The Mummy* [of Rameses II] *was met at Orly airport by Mme Saunier-Seïté.*
– News item, Sept. 1976)

– May I welcome Your Majesty to Paris.

– Mm.

– I hope the flight from Cairo was reasonable.

– Mmmmm.

– We have a germ-proof room at the Museum of Man
  where we trust Your Majesty will have peace and quiet.

– Unh-unh.

– I am sorry, but this is necessary.
  Your Majesty's person harbours a fungus.

– Fng fng's, hn?

– Well, it is something attacking your cells.
  Your Majesty is gently deteriorating
  after nearly four thousand years
  becalmed in masterly embalmment.
  We wish to save you from the worm.

– Wrm hrm! Mgh-mgh-mgh.

– Indeed I know it must be distressing
  to a pharaoh and a son of Ra,
  to the excavator of Abu Simbel
  that glorious temple in the rock,
  to the perfecter of Karnak hall,
  to the hammer of the Hittites,
  to the colossus whose colossus
  raised in red granite at holy Thebes
  sixteen-men-high astounds the desert
  shattered, as Your Majesty in life
  shattered the kingdom and oppressed the poor
  with such lavish grandeur and panache,

114

to Rameses, to Ozymandias,
to the Louis Quatorze of the Nile,
how bitter it must be to feel
a microbe eat your camphored bands.
But we are here to help Your Majesty.
We shall encourage you to unwind.
You have many useful years ahead.

– M' n'm 'z 'zym'ndias, kng'v kngz!

– Yes yes. Well, Shelley is dead now.
He was not embalmed. He will not write
about Your Majesty again.

– T't'nkh'm'n? H'tsh'ps't?
'khn't'n N'f'rt'ti? Mm? Mm?

– The hall of fame has many mansions.
Your Majesty may rest assured
your deeds will always be remembered.

– Youmm w'm'nn. B't'f'lll w'm'nnnn.
No w'm'nnn f'r th'zndz y'rz.

– Your Majesty, what are you doing?

– Ng! Mm. Mhm. Mm? Mm? Mmmmm.

– Your Majesty, Your Majesty! You'll break your stitches!

– Fng st'chez fng's wrm hrm.

– I really hate to have to use
a hypodermic on a mummy,
but we cannot have you strain yourself.
Remember your fungus, Your Majesty.

– Fng. Zzzzzzzz.

– That's right.

– Aaaaaaaaah.

Instructions to an Actor

Now, boy, remember this is the great scene.
You'll stand on a pedestal behind a curtain,
the curtain will be drawn, and then you don't move
for eighty lines; don't move, don't speak, don't breathe.
I'll stun them all out there, I'll scare them,
make them weep, but it depends on you.
I warn you eighty lines is a long time,
but you don't breathe, you're dead,
you're a dead queen, a statue,
you're dead as stone, new-carved,
new-painted and the paint not dry
– we'll get some red to keep your lip shining –
and you're a mature woman, you've got dignity,
some beauty still in middle age, and
you're kind and true, but you're dead,
your husband thinks you're dead,
the audience thinks you're dead,
and you don't breathe, boy, I say
you don't even blink for eighty lines,
if you blink you're out!
Fix your eye on something and keep watching it.
Practise when you get home. It can be done.
And you move at last – music's the cue.
When you hear a mysterious solemn jangle
of instruments, make yourself ready.
Five lines more, you can lift a hand.
It may tingle a bit, but lift it –
slow, slow –
O this is where I hit them
right between the eyes, I've got them now –
I'm making the dead walk –
you move a foot, slow, steady, down,
you guard your balance in case you're stiff,
you move, you step down, down from the pedestal,
control your skirt with one hand, the other hand
you now hold out –
O this will melt their hearts if nothing does –
to your husband who wronged you long ago
and hesitates in amazement
to believe you are alive.

116

Finally he embraces you, and there's nothing
I can give you to say, boy,
but you must show that you have forgiven him.
Forgiveness, that's the thing. It's like a second life.
I know you can do it. – Right then, shall we try?

Migraine Attack

We had read about the reed-beds but went on
right through the night. With blades as sharp as that
you scarcely feel the cuts, and blood in darkness
is merely darkness. Oh there was moonlight
in fits and starts, but it confused us more
than it ever illuminated, as we kept moving
under the jagged filter of the forest ceiling –
whatever light there was made convicts of us,
frisked us, left us stumbling through our chains
of shadows. From our feet – shadows,
from our rifles – shadows, from branches –
shadows like bats and bats like shadows.
Sometimes the treetop mat was thick with mosses,
creepers, ancient nests, a stamping-ground
for upside-down explorers going to heaven:
we really saw them there, in our delirium,
riding on giant sloths, with their rags of clothes
and raddled hair streaming down to gravity.
They passed; the scrunts and scrogs passed; snakes passed;
eyes and beaks in bushes passed; a long wing passed;
the scuttlings and the slitherings and the roars
passed; time, even, as they passed, must have passed.
We were moving columns of sweat and crusted blood,
burrs, leaf-mould, mud, mosquitoes, map-cases
and a bandage or two as we leaned into it
to defeat it, and the wood grew grey
as it gave up and felt
the distant day, thinned out
to glades threaded by mist
sent from the unseen sun.
We shook ourselves like dogs
and tried a song.

117

Winter

The year goes, the woods decay, and after,
many a summer dies. The swan
on Bingham's pond, a ghost, comes and goes.
It goes, and ice appears, it holds,
bears gulls that stand around surprised,
blinking in the heavy light, bears boys
when skates take over, the swan-white ice
glints only crystal beyond white. Even
dearest blue's not there, though poets would find it.
I find one stark scene
cut by evening cries, by warring air.
The muffled hiss of blades escapes into breath,
hangs with it a moment, fades off.
Fades off, goes, the scene, the voices fade,
the line of trees, the woods that fall, decay
and break, the dark comes down, the shouts
run off into it and disappear.
At last the lamps go too, when fog
drives monstrous down the dual carriageway
out to the west, and even in my room
and on this paper I do not know
about that grey dead pane
of ice that sees nothing and that nothing sees.

Surrealism Revisited

An avuncular mussel stamped its foot and the sea took an attack
    of vertigo as far as it would go.
A dictionary without happiness was shot down as it gave a perfect
    bound over the heights of hands.
A caryatid ate a parrot with traffic jam.
A penthouse laid a bad egg and the prime minister took it to the
    country.
A crate of brandy snaps was driven mad by a strike of cream.
A giant wheel was arrested for blasphemy as it tried to thread a
    needle.

An interurban flyover turned into an old hag in broad daylight
    and was dismembered by cranes.
A bag of sleet was found in a blast furnace.
An ant's egg filled with speculators was detonated by remote
    control.
A silver centaur ridden by a golden boy plunged through the sky
    screaming for paint-stripper.
A clockwork orange by Fabergé fell out of a magpie's nest and ate
    humble pie.
A brazen yelp escaped from a condemned gasholder and was torn
    to pieces in a fight between scavengers and demons.
A book two miles high with phosphorescent letters in an unknown
    language stopped shipping in the channel for four days.
A cat barked and was deported.

On the Water

There is something almost but not quite
beguiling about the thought of houseboat days.
Creaking, lapping, a sense of sway and the illusion
of moving might be the romance of a weekend.
Toy cabins, timeless horizontal afternoons
might at last get through Proust, while she
reverses roles at a punchbag on the deck,
knocks herself groggy, takes to cushions
as the sun goes down. These scenes
would only be for laughter though. Who is to make
the omelette, the one with throbbing shoulder or
the one dozy-eyed from Combray
on his back with a paper-knife,
reading against the light? The strenuous things
are great gods, bored by windows giving on water,
and even pretty hands trailed in water
knit nothing, and ask nothing to be done.
Life came from seas, lakes? It must be a joke.
The sluggish firth, like the latest bandage,
melts into the body of the earth,
cannot even sustain conversation.

It would be a breach to crow over a slammed chessman,
let alone slot in the Flying Dutchman cassette
they'd be sure to pack, these chained wanderers.
They dream, in fits and starts; it is only then
that the boat drifts, right down
to the sea and the keen wind, only then
that great gods clap their wings, and he designs
an airport, she a house and
a dress she stands in at the door to welcome
many guests and set parties ablaze.

On the Needle's Point

Of course it is not a point at all.
We live here, and we should know.
I doubt indeed if there can be a point
in created things: the finest honing
uncovers more rough. Our ground stretches
for several miles, it is like living
on an asteroid, a bounded island
but with a bottomless core lost in mist
so far below and out of sight we feel
like pillar saints in earthly Syria.
The surface is slashed and pitted, greyish
with streaks of black and enigmatic
blue silver; spores of red lichen
gather and smoulder in crevices and caves.
At the edge it is very prodigious.
We have had some climbing over and down
with home-made crampons, disappearing,
perhaps making it to what we cannot imagine,
others fly off with fixed smiles,
vanish in their elation into violet haze.
But I like it on the point, good
is the dark cavern, good the craggy walks,
good the vertiginous bare brightness,
good the music, good the dance

when sometimes we join wings and drift
in interlinking circles, how many thousands
I could never tell, silent ourselves,
almost melting into light.

The Coals

Before my mother's hysterectomy
she cried, and told me she must never bring
coals in from the cellar outside the house,
someone must do it for her. The thing itself
I knew was nothing, it was the thought
of that dependence. Her tears shocked me
like a blow. As once she had been taught,
I was taught self-reliance, discipline,
which is both good and bad. You get things done,
you feel you keep the waste and darkness back
by acts and acts and acts and acts and acts,
bridling if someone tells you this is vain,
learning at last in pain. Hardest of all
is to forgive yourself for things undone,
guilt that can poison life – away with it,
you say, and it is loath to go away.
I learned both love and joy in a hard school
and treasure them like the fierce salvage of
some wreck that has been built to look like stone
and stand, though it did not, a thousand years.

Little Blue Blue

(misprinted title of Norman MacCaig's poem
'Little Boy Blue' in *The Equal Skies*, 1980)

The mirror caught him as he straightened his sky-blue tie,
he was the son of sky and sea, five
feet high with wings furled, flexing
and shifting the sheen of his midnight blue
mohair tuxedo, tightening his saxe plastic belt
one notch, slicing the room with Gillette-blue eyes,
padding to the door in dove-blue brushed suede boots,
pinning his buttonhole periwinkle with a blue shark's grin.

> Once in the street
> he got the beat
> unfurled his wing
> began to sing
> 'She is, he is, she is my star'
> to his electric blue guitar.

Little Blue Blue flew to the land of denim,
bought himself jeans and a denim jacket and a denim cap,
what blue, what blue, he cried, and tried his jeans
with his mohair dinner-jacket, tried his mohair trousers
with his denim bomber jacket, tried his denim cap
with his saxe-blue belt and his dove-blue boots and a
navy-blue Adidas bag and nothing else
till the slate-blue pigeons all blushed purple, but

> once in the street
> he got the beat
> unfurled his wing
> began to sing
> 'He is, she is, he is my star'
> to his electric blue guitar.

Then he went to sea and sailed the blue main
in his navy jersey with his wings well battened down,
knocked up a tattoo parlour in old Yokohama,
got bluebirds on his hands and a blue pierced heart,
and a geisha-girl on his shoulder with a blue rose,
and a trail of blue hounds chasing a blue fox

into covert – oh, he said, I'm black and blue all over,
but he staggered out into that Nippon moon, and

> once in the street
> he got the beat
> unfurled his wing
> began to sing
> 'She is, he is, she is my star'
> to his electric blue guitar.

Back home, he bought a cobalt Talbot Sunbeam
with aquamarine upholstery and citizens band radio,
said Blue Blue here, do you read me, do you read me?
as he whizzed up to Scrabster in his royal-blue pinstripes.
And his dashboard sent him messages without measure,
for everybody loves a blue angel, whistling
at the wheel under azure highland skies.
And he stopped at each village, and smiled like the sun, for

> once in the street
> he got the beat
> unfurled his wing
> began to sing
> 'He is, she is, he is my star'
> to his electric blue guitar.

Grendel

It is being nearly human
gives me this spectacular darkness.
The light does not know what to do with me.
I rise like mist and I go down like water.
I saw them soused with wine behind their windows.
I watched them making love, twisting like snakes.
I heard a blind man pick the strings, and sing.
There are torches everywhere, there are faces
swimming in shine and sweat and beer and grins and greed.
There are tapers confusing the stacked spears.

There are queens on their knees at idols, crosses, lamps.
There are handstand clowns knocked headlong by maudlin heroes.
There are candles in the sleazy bowers, the whores
sleep all day with mice across their feet.
The slung warhorn gleams in the drizzle,
the horses shift their hooves and shiver.
It is all a pestilence, life within life
and movement within movement, lips meeting,
grooming of mares, roofs plated with gold,
hunted pelts laid on kings,
neck-veins bursting from greasy torques,
pouches of coins gamed off, slaves and outlaws
eating hailstones under heaven.
Who would be a man? Who would be the winter sparrow
that flies at night by mistake into a lighted hall
and flutters the length of it in zigzag panic,
dazed and terrified by the heat and noise and smoke,
the drink-fumes and the oaths, the guttering flames,
feast-bones thrown to a snarl of wolfhounds,
flash of swords in sodden sorry quarrels,
till at last he sees the other door
and skims out in relief and joy
into the stormy dark?
– Black grove, black lake, black sky,
no shoe or keel or wing undoes your stillness
as I plod through the fens and prowl
in my own place and sometimes stand many hours, as now,
above those unreflecting waters, reflecting as I can
on men, and on their hideous clamorous brilliance
that beats the ravens' beaks into the ground
and douses a million funeral pyres.

Jack London in Heaven

Part the clouds, let me look down.
Oh god that earth. A breeze comes from the sea
and humpback fogs blanch off to blindness, the sun
hits Frisco, it shines solid up to heaven.

I can't bear not to see a brisk day on the Bay,
it drives me out of my mind but I can't bear
not to watch the choppy waters, Israfel.
I got a sea-eagle once to come up here
screaming and turn a prayer-wheel or two
with angry buffets till the sharpshooters
sent him to hell, and I groaned,
grew dark with disfavour. – What,
I should pray now? For these thoughts?
Here are some more. I was up at four
for psalms, shawms, smarms, salaams, yessirs, yesmaams,
felt-tipped hosannas melting into mist,
a mushroom high, an elation of vapours,
a downpour of dumpy amens. Azazel,
I am sick of fireflies. It's a dumb joss.
– You know I'm a spoilt angel? What happens to us?
I'm not so bright – or bright, perhaps. God knows!
They almost let me fall through heaven craning
to see sunshine dappling the heaving gunmetal
of the Oakland Estuary – the crawl, the swell, the crests
I could pull up to touch and wet my hands
let down a moment into time and space.
How long will they allow me to remember
as I pick the cloud-rack apart and peer?
The estuary, Israfel, the glittering estuary, August '96!
My last examination has scratched to a finish,
I'm rushing to the door, whooping and squawking,
I dance down the steps, throw my hat in the air
as the dusty invigilator frowns, gathers in
that furious harvest of four months' cramming,
nineteen hours a day – my vigils, Azazel,
my holy vigils – the oyster-pirate hammering
at the gates of the state university.
It's enough. I got in. But at that time
I took a boat out on the ebb
to be alone where no book ever was.
I scudded dreaming through the creamy rings
of light and water, followed the shore
and thought of earth and heaven and myself
till I saw a shipyard I knew, and the delta rushes
and the weeds and the tin wharves, and smelt the ropes
and some tobacco-smoke, and longed for company.

– Evensong? I'm not coming to evensong.
Get off, get away. Go on, sing for your supper!
Bloody angels! – So I sailed in, made fast,
and there was Charley, and Liz, and Billy and Joe, and Dutch
– that desperate handsome godlike drunken man –
old friends, Azazel, old friends that clambered over me
and sang and wept and filled me with whisky and beer
brought teetering across the railroad tracks
all that long noon.
They would have kept me there, oh, for ever
but I could see the blue through the open door,
that blue, my sea, and they knew
I had to be away, and got me stumbling down the wharf steps
into a good salmon boat, with charcoal and a brazier
and coffee and a pot and a pan and a fresh-caught fish
and cast me off into a stiff wind.
I tell you, Israfel, the sea was white
and half of it was in my boat
with my sail set hard like a board.
Everything whipped and cracked
in pure green glory as
I stood braced at the mast
and roared out 'Shenandoah'.
Did Odysseus get to heaven?
I came down to earth, at Antioch,
sobered in the sunset shadows, tied up
alongside a potato sloop, had friends
aboard there too, who sizzled my fish for me
and gave me stew and crusty bread and claret,
claret in great pint mugs, and wrapped me in blankets
warmer and softer than the clouds of heaven.
What did we not talk of as we smoked,
sea-tales Odysseus might have known,
under the same night wind, the same wild rigging.
– Azazel, I must get down there!
I am a wasting shade, I am drifting and dying
by these creeping streams. If you are my friend,
tell them my trouble. Tell them
they cannot make me a heaven
like the tide-race and the tiller
and a broken-nailed hand
and the shrouds of Frisco.

Cinquevalli

Cinquevalli is falling, falling.
The shining trapeze kicks and flirts free,
solo performer at last.
The sawdust puffs up with a thump,
settles on a tangle of broken limbs.
St Petersburg screams and leans.
His pulse flickers with the gas-jets. He lives.

Cinquevalli has a therapy.
In his hospital bed, in his hospital chair
he holds a ball, lightly, lets it roll round his hand,
or grips it tight, gauging its weight and resistance,
begins to balance it, to feel its life attached to his
by will and knowledge, invisible strings
that only he can see. He throws it
from hand to hand, always different,
always the same, always
different, always the
same.
His muscles learn to think, his arms grow very strong.

Cinquevalli in sepia
looks at me from an old postcard: bundle of enigmas.
Half faun, half military man; almond eyes, curly hair,
conventional moustache; tights, and a tunic loaded
with embroideries, tassels, chains, fringes; hand on hip
with a large signet-ring winking at the camera
but a bull neck and shoulders and a cannon-ball
at his elbow as he stands by the posing pedestal;
half reluctant, half truculent,
half handsome, half absurd,
but let me see you forget him: not to be done.

Cinquevalli is a juggler.
In a thousand theatres, in every continent,
he is the best, the greatest. After eight years perfecting
he can balance one billiard ball on another billiard ball
on top of a cue on top of a third billiard ball
in a wine-glass held in his mouth. To those
who say the balls are waxed, or flattened,

127

he patiently explains the trick will only work
because the spheres are absolutely true.
There is no deception in him. He is true.

Cinquevalli is juggling with a bowler,
a walking-stick, a cigar, and a coin.
Who foresees? How to please.
The last time round, the bowler
flies to his head, the stick sticks in his hand,
the cigar jumps into his mouth, the coin
lands on his foot – ah, but
is kicked into his eye
and held there as the miraculous monocle
without which the portrait would be incomplete.

Cinquevalli is practising.
He sits in his dressing-room talking to some friends,
at the same time writing a letter with one hand
and with the other juggling four balls.
His friends think of demons, but
'You could all do this,' he says,
sealing the letter with a billiard ball.

Cinquevalli is on the high wire in Odessa.
The roof cracks, he is falling, falling
into the audience, a woman breaks his fall,
he cracks her like a flea, but lives.

Cinquevalli broods in his armchair in Brixton Road.
He reads in the paper about the shells whining
at Passchendaele, imagines the mud and the dead.
He goes to the window and wonders through that dark evening
what is happening in Poland where he was born.
His neighbours call him a German spy.
'Kestner, Paul Kestner, that's his name!'
'Keep Kestner out of the British music-hall!'
He frowns; it is cold; his fingers seem stiff and old.

Cinquevalli tosses up a plate of soup
and twirls it on his forefinger; not a drop spills.
He laughs, and well may he laugh
who can do that. The astonished table

breathe again, laugh too, think the world
a spinning thing that spills, for a moment, no drop.

Cinquevalli's coffin sways through Brixton
only a few months before the Armistice.
Like some trick they cannot get off the ground
it seems to burden the shuffling bearers, all their arms
cross-juggle that displaced person, that man
of balance, of strength, of delights and marvels,
in his unsteady box at last into the earth.

Sonnets from Scotland

O Wechsel der Zeiten! Du Hoffnung des Volks!
                                                    Brecht

SLATE

There is no beginning. We saw Lewis
laid down, when there was not much but thunder
and volcanic fires; watched long seas plunder
faults; laughed as Staffa cooled. Drumlins blue as
bruises were grated off like nutmegs; bens,
and a great glen, gave a rough back we like
to think the ages must streak, surely strike,
seldom stroke, but raised and shaken, with tens
of thousands of rains, blizzards, sea-poundings
shouldered off into night and memory.
Memory of men! That was to come. Great
in their empty hunger these surroundings
threw walls to the sky, the sorry glory
of a rainbow. Their heels kicked flint, chalk, slate.

CARBONIFEROUS
For I.R.

Diving in the warm seas around Bearsden,
cased in our superchitin scuba-gear,
we found a world so wonderfully clear
it seemed a heaven given there and then.
Hardly! *Et in Arcadia*, said the shark,
ego. We stumbled on a nest of them.
How could bright water that hid nothing stem
our ancient shudder? They themselves were dark,
but all we saw was the unsinister
ferocious tenderness of mating shapes,
a raking love that scoured their skin to shreds.
We feared instead the force that could inter
such life and joy, in fossil clays, for apes
and men to haul into their teeming heads.

POST-GLACIAL

The glaciers melt slowly in the sun.
The ice groans as it shrinks back to the pole.
Loud splits and cracks send shudders through the shoal
of herring struggling northwards, but they run
steadily on into the unknown roads
and the whole stream of life runs with them. Brown
islands hump up in the white of land, down
in the valleys a fresh drained greenness loads
fields like a world first seen, and when mild rains
drive back the blizzards, a new world it is
of grain that thrusts its frenzied spikes, and trees
whose roots race under the stamped-out remains
of nomad Grampian fires. Immensities
are mind, not ice, as the bright straths unfreeze.

IN ARGYLL
For A.R.

We found the poet's skull on the machair.
It must have bobbed ashore from that shipwreck
where the winged men went down in rolling dreck
of icebound webs, oars, oaths, armour, blind air.
It watches westward still; dry, white as chalk,
perfect at last, in silence and at rest.
Far off, he sang of Nineveh the blest,
incised his tablets, stalked the dhow-bright dock.
Now he needs neither claws nor tongue to tell
of things undying. Hebridean light
fills the translucent bone-domes. Nothing brings
the savage brain back to its empty shell,
distracted by the shouts, the reefs, the night,
fighting sleet to fix the tilt of its wings.

THE RING OF BRODGAR

'If those stones could speak –' Do not wish too loud.
They can, they do, they will. No voice is lost.
Your meanest guilts are bonded in like frost.
Your fearsome sweat will rise and leave its shroud.

I well recall the timeprint of the Ring
of Brodgar we discovered, white with dust
in twenty-second-century distrust
of truth, but dustable, with truths to bring
into the freer ages, as it did.
A thin groan fought the wind that tugged the stones.
It filled an auditorium with pain.
Long was the sacrifice. Pity ran, hid.
Once they heard the splintering of the bones
they switched the playback off, in vain, in vain.

SILVA CALEDONIA

The darkness deepens, and the woods are long.
We shall never see any stars. We thought
we heard a horn a while back, faintly brought
through barks and howls, the nearest to a song
you ever heard in these grey dripping glens.
But if there were hunters, we saw not one.
Are there bears? Mist. Wolves? Peat. Is there a sun?
Where are the eyes that should peer from those dens?
Marsh-lights, yes, mushroom-banks, leaf-mould, rank ferns,
and up above, a sense of wings, of flight,
of clattering, of calls through fog. Yet men,
going about invisible concerns,
are here, and our immoderate delight
waits to see them, and hear them speak, again.

PILATE AT FORTINGALL

A Latin harsh with Aramaicisms
poured from his lips incessantly; it made
no sense, for surely he was mad. The glade
of birches shamed his rags, in paroxysms
he stumbled, toga'd, furred, blear, brittle, grey.
They told us he sat here beneath the yew
even in downpours; ate dog-scraps. Crows flew
from prehistoric stone to stone all day.

132

'See him now.' He crawled to the cattle-trough
at dusk, jumbled the water till it sloshed
and spilled into the hoof-mush in blue strands,
slapped with useless despair each sodden cuff,
and washed his hands, and watched his hands, and washed
his hands, and watched his hands, and washed his hands.

THE MIRROR

There is a mirror only we can see.
It hangs in time and not in space. The day
goes down in it without ember or ray
and the newborn climb through it to be free.
The multitudes of the world cannot know
they are reflected there; like glass they lie
in glass, shadows in shade, they could not cry
in airless wastes but that is where they go.
We cloud it, but it pulses like a gem,
it must have caught a range of energies
from the dead. We breathe again; nothing shows.
Back in space, *ubi solitudinem*
faciunt pacem appellant. Ages
drum-tap the flattened homes and slaughtered rows.

THE PICTS

Names as from outer space, names without roots:
Bes, son of Nanammovvezz; Bliesblituth
that wild buffoon throned in an oaken booth;
wary Edarnon; brilliant Usconbuts;
Canutulachama who read the stars.
Where their fame flashed from, went to, is unknown.
The terror of their warriors is known,
naked, tattooed on every part (the hairs
of the groin are shaved on greatest fighters,
the fine bone needle dipped in dark-blue woad
rings the flesh with tender quick assurance:
he is *diuperr cartait*, rich pin; writers
like us regain mere pain on that blue road,
they think honour comes with the endurance).

133

COLLOQUY IN GLASCHU

God but *le son du cor*, Columba sighed
to Kentigern, *est triste au fond silvarum!*
Frater, said Kentigern, I see no harm.
J'aime le son du cor, when day has died,
deep in the *bois*, and oystercatchers rise
before the fowler as he trudges home
and *sermo lupi* loosens the grey loam.
À l'horizon lointain is paradise,
abest silentium, le cor éclate –
– *et meurt*, Columba mused, but Kentigern
replied, *renaît et se prolonge*. The cell
is filled with song. Outside, *puer cantat*.
Veni venator sings the gallus kern.
The saints dip startled cups in Mungo's well.

MEMENTO

over the cliff-top and into the mist
across the heather and down to the peat
here with the sheep and where with the peeweet
through the stubble and by the pheasant's tryst
above the pines and past the northern lights
along the voe and out to meet the ice
among the stacks and round their kreidekreis
in summer lightning and beneath white nights
behind the haar and in front of the tower
beyond the moor and against writ and ring
below the mort-gate and outwith all kind
under the hill and at the boskless bower
over the hills and far away to bring
over the hills and far away to mind

MATTHEW PARIS

'North and then north and north again we sailed,
not that God is in the north or the south
but that the north is great and strange, a mouth
of baleen filtering the unknown, veiled

spoutings and sportings, curtains of white cold.
I made a map, I made a map of it.
Here I have bristly Scotland, almost split
in two, what sea-lochs and rough marches, old
forts, new courts, when Alexander their king
is dead will they live in love and peace, get
bearings, trace mountains, count stars, take capes, straits
in their stride as well as crop and shop, bring
luck home? *Pelagus vastissimum et
invium*, their element, my margin, waits.'

AT STIRLING CASTLE, 1507

Damian, D'Amiens, Damiano –
we never found out his true name, but there
he crouched, swarthy, and slowly sawed the air
with large strapped-on bat-membrane wings. Below
the battlements, a crowd prepared to jeer.
He frowned, moved back, and then with quick crow struts
ran forward, flapping strongly, whistling cuts
from the grey heavy space with his black gear
and on a huge spring and a cry was out
beating into vacancy, three, four, five,
till the crawling scaly Forth and the rocks
and the upturned heads replaced that steel shout
of sky he had replied to – left alive,
and not the last key snapped from high hard locks.

THOMAS YOUNG, M.A. (ST ANDREWS)
For J.C.B.

'Yes, I taught Milton. He was a sharp boy.
He never understood predestination,
but then who does, within the English nation?
I did my best to let him see what joy
there must be in observing the damnation
of those whom God makes truly reprobate:
the fair percentage does not decreate
heaven, but gives all angels the elation

135

they are justly decreed to have deserved.
We took a short tour up to Auchterarder,
where there are strong sound sergeants of the creed,
but John could only ask how God was served
by those who neither stand nor wait, their ardour
rabid (he said) to expunge virtue's seed?'

LADY GRANGE ON ST KILDA

'They say I'm mad, but who would not be mad
on Hirta, when the winter raves along
the bay and howls through my stone hut, so strong
they thought I was and so I am, so bad
they thought I was and beat me black and blue
and banished me, my mouth of bloody teeth
and banished me to live and cry beneath
the shriek of sea-birds, and eight children too
we had, my lord, though I know what you are,
sleekit Jacobite, showed you up, you bitch,
and screamed outside your close at Niddry's Wynd,
until you set your men on me, and far
I went from every friend and solace, which
was cruel, out of mind, out of my mind.'

THEORY OF THE EARTH

James Hutton that true son of fire who said
to Burns 'Aye, man, the rocks melt wi the sun'
was sure the age of reason's time was done:
what but imagination could have read
granite boulders back to their molten roots?
And how far back was back, and how far on
would basalt still be basalt, iron iron?
Would second seas re-drown the fossil brutes?
'We find no vestige of a beginning,
no prospect of an end.' They died almost
together, poet and geologist,
and lie in wait for hilltop buoys to ring,
or aw the seas gang dry and Scotland's coast
dissolve in crinkled sand and pungent mist.

136

POE IN GLASGOW

The sun beat on the Moby-Dick-browed boy.
It was a day to haunt the Broomielaw.
The smell of tar, the slap of water, draw
his heart out from the wharf in awe and joy.
Oh, not Virginia, not Liverpool –
and not the Isle of Dogs or Greenwich Reach –
but something through the masts – a blue – a beach –
an inland gorge of rivers green and cool.
'Wake up!' a sailor coiled with bright rope cried
and almost knocked him off his feet, making
towards his ship. 'You want to serve your time
as cabin-boy's assistant, eh?' The ride
and creak of wood comes home, testing, shaking.
'Where to?' He laughed. 'To Arnheim, boy, Arnheim!'

DE QUINCEY IN GLASGOW

Twelve thousand drops of laudanum a day
kept him from shrieking. Wrapped in a duffle
buttoned to the neck, he made his shuffle,
door, table, window, table, door, bed, lay
on bed, sighed, groaned, jumped from bed, sat and wrote
till the table was white with pages, rang
for his landlady, ordered mutton, sang
to himself with pharmacies in his throat.
When afternoons grew late, he feared and longed
for dusk. In that high room in Rottenrow
he looks out east to the Necropolis.
Its crowded tombs rise jostling, living, thronged
with shadows, and the granite-bloodying glow
flares on the dripping bronze of a used kris.

PETER GUTHRIE TAIT, TOPOLOGIST

Leith dock's lashed spars roped the young heart of Tait.
What made gales tighten, not undo, each knot?
Nothing's more dazzling than a ravelling plot.
Stubby crisscrossing fingers fixed the freight

so fast he started sketching on the spot.
The mathematics of the twisted state
uncoiled its waiting elegances, straight.
Old liquid chains that strung the gorgeous tot
God spliced the mainbrace with, put on the slate,
and sent creation reeling from, clutched hot
as caustic on Tait's brain when he strolled late
along the links and saw the stars had got
such gouts and knots of well-tied fire the mate
must sail out whistling to his stormy lot.

G.M. HOPKINS IN GLASGOW
For J.A.M.R.

Earnestly nervous yet forthright, melted
by bulk and warmth and unimposed rough grace,
he lit a ready fuse from face to face
of Irish Glasgow. Dark tough tight-belted
drunken Fenian poor ex-Ulstermen
crouched round a brazier like a burning bush
and lurched into his soul with such a push
that British angels blanched in mid-amen
to see their soldier stumble like a Red.
Industry's pauperism singed his creed.
He blessed them, frowned, beat on his hands. The load
of coal-black darkness clattering on his head
half-crushed, half-fed the bluely burning need
that trudged him back along North Woodside Road.

1893
For P. McC.

A Slav philosopher in Stronachlachar:
Vladimir Solovyov looked down the loch.
The sun was shimmering on birk and sauch.
'This beats the fishy vennels of St Machar,'
he said, and added, 'Inversnaid tomorrow!'
A boatman rowing to him from infinity
turned out to be a boatwoman. 'Divinity!'
he cried, 'shake back your hair, and shake back sorrow!'

138

The boat was grounded, she walked past him singing.
To her, he was a man of forty, reading.
Within him the words mounted: 'Sing for me,
dancing like Wisdom before the Lord, bringing
your mazy unknown waters with you, seeding
the Northern Lights and churning up the sea!'

THE TICKET

'There are two rivers: how can a drop go
from one stream to the next?' Gurdjieff was asked.
The unflummoxable master stretched, basked.
'It must buy a ticket,' he said. A row
of demons dragged the Inaccessible
Pinnacle through the centre of Glasgow,
barking out sweaty orders, pledged to show
it was bloody juggernaut-time, able
to jam shrieking children under crashed spires.
But soon that place began to recompose,
the film ran back, the walls stood, the cries died,
the demons faded to familiar fires.
In New York, Gurdjieff changed his caftan, chose
a grape, sat, smiled. 'They never paid their ride.'

NORTH AFRICA

Why did the poets come to the desert?
They learned the meaning of an oasis,
the meaning of heat, fellahin's phrases,
tents behind the khamsin-blasted dannert.
We watched MacLean at the Ruweisat Ridge
giving a piercing look as he passed by
the fly-buzzed grey-faced dead; swivelled our eye
west through tank-strewn dune and strafed-out village
with Henderson; and Hay saw Bizerta
burn; Garioch was taken at Tobruk,
parched *Kriegsgefangener*, calm, reading *Shveik*;
Morgan ate sand, slept sand at El Ballah
while gangrened limbs dropped in the pail; Farouk
fed Fraser memorandums like a shrike.

CALEDONIAN ANTISYZYGY

– Knock knock. – Who's there? – Doctor. – Doctor Who? – No,
just Doctor. – What's up Doc? – Stop, that's all cock.
– O.K. – Knock knock. – Who's there? – Doctor Who. – Doc-
tor Who who? – Doctor, who's a silly schmo?
– Right. Out! – Aw. – Well, last chance, come on. – Knock knock.
– Who's there? – Doctor Jekyll. – Doctor Jekyll
who? – Doctor, 'd ye kill Mr Hyde? – Pig-swill!
Nada! Rubbish! Lies! Garbage! Never! Schlock!
– Calm down, your turn. – Knock knock. – Who's there? – Doctor
Knox. – Doctor Knox who? – Doctor Knocks Box Talks.
Claims T.V. Favours Grim Duo, Burke, Hare.
– Right, join hands. Make sure the door is locked, or
nothing will happen. – Dark yet? – Cover clocks.
– Knock. – Listen! – Is there anybody there?

TRAVELLERS (1)

The universe is like a trampoline.
We chose a springy clump near Arrochar
and with the first jump shot past Barnard's Star.
The universe is like a tambourine.
We clashed a brace of planets as we swung
some rolling unknown ringing system up
above our heads, and kicked it too. To sup,
sleep, recoup, we dropped to the House of Tongue.
The universe is like a trampoline.
Tongue threw us into a satellite bank.
We photographed a mole; a broch; the moon.
The universe is like a tambourine.
We stretched out, shook Saturn, its janglings sank
and leapt till it was neither night nor noon.

TRAVELLERS (2)

As it was neither night nor noon, we mused
a bit, dissolved ourselves a bit, took stock,
folded the play away and turned the lock.
Exhilarated travellers unused

to feeling blank can love the nescience
of a stilled moment. Undenied the time,
a lingering, a parasol, a lime.
There is no happiness in prescience,
and there is no regret in happiness.
A coast swept out in headlands and was lost.
And there we could have left the thought unthought
or hope undrafted, but that a bright press
of lights showed where a distant liner crossed.
Its horn blew through us, urgent, deep, unsought.

SEFERIS ON EIGG

The isles of Scotland! the isles of Scotland!
But Byron sang elsewhere; loved, died elsewhere.
Seferis stiffly cupped warm blue May air
and slowly sifted it from hand to hand.
It was good and Greek. Amazed to find it,
he thought the dancing sea, the larks, the boats
spoke out as clear as from Aegean throats.
What else there was – he might half-unwind it.
One day he visited the silent cave
where Walter Scott, that tawdry Ulysses,
purloined a suffocated clansman's skull.
Crowns of Scottish kings were sacred; the lave
can whistle for dignity – who misses
them, peasants, slaves? Greeks, too, could shrug the cull.

MATT McGINN

We cannot see it, it keeps changing so.
All round us, *in and out, above, below,*
at evening, *phantom figures come and go,*
silently, *just a magic shadow show.*
A hoarse voice singing *come love watch with me*
was all we heard on that fog-shrouded bank.
We thought we saw him, but if so, he sank
into the irrecoverable sea.
Dear merry man, what is your country now?
Does it keep changing? Will we ever see it?

A crane, a backcourt, an accordion?
Or sherbet dabs, henna, and jasmined brow?
The book is clasped, and time will never free it.
Mektub. The caravan winds jangling on.

POST-REFERENDUM

'No no, it will not do, it will not be.
I tell you you must leave your land alone.
Who do you think is poised to ring the phone?
Fish your straitjacket packet from the sea
you threw it in, get your headphones mended.
You don't want the world now, do you? Come on,
you're pegged out on your heathery futon,
take the matches from your lids, it's ended.'
We watched the strong sick dirkless Angel groan,
shiver, half-rise, batter with a shrunk wing
the space the Tempter was no longer in.
He tried to hear feet, calls, car-doors, shouts, drone
of engines, hooters, hear a meeting sing.
A coin clattered at the end of its spin.

GANGS

Naw naw, there's nae big wurds here, there ye go.
Christ man ye're in a bad wey, kin ye staun?
See here noo, wance we know jist where we're gaun,
we'll jump thon auld – stoap that, will ye – *Quango*.
Thaim that squealt *Lower Inflation*, aye, thaim,
plus thae *YY Zero Wage Increase* wans,
they'll no know what hit thim. See yours, and Dan's,
and mine's, that's three chibs. We'll soon hiv a team.
Whit's that? *Non-Index-Linked!* Did ye hear it?
Look! *Tiny Global Recession!* C'moan then,
ya bams, Ah'll take ye. *Market Power fae Drum!*
Dave, man, get up. Dave! Ach, ye're no near it.
Ah'm oan ma tod. But they'll no take a len
a me, Ah'm no deid yet, or deif, or dumb!

AFTER A DEATH

A writer needs nothing but a table.
His pencil races, pauses, crosses out.
Five years ago he lost his friend, without
him he struggles through a different fable.
The one who died, he is the better one.
The other one is selfish, ruthless, he
uses people, floats in an obscure sea
of passions, half-drowns as the livid sun
goes down, calls out for help he will not give.
Examine yourself! He is afraid to.
But that is not quite true, I saw him look
into that terrible place, let him live
at least with what is eternally due
to love that lies in earth in cold Carluke.

NOT THE BURRELL COLLECTION

The Buenos Aires Vase, one mile across,
flickering with unsleeping silent flames,
its marble carved in vine-leaves mixed with names,
shirtless ones and *desaparecidos*;
a collier's iron collar, riveted,
stamped by his Burntisland owner; a spade
from Babiy Yar; a blood-crust from the blade
that jumped the corpse of Wallace for his head;
the stout rack soaked in Machiavelli's sweat;
a fire-circled scorpion; a blown frog;
the siege of Beirut in stained glass; a sift
of Auschwitz ash; an old tapestry-set
unfinished, with a crowd, a witch, a log;
a lachrymatory no man can lift.

1983

'A parrot Edward Lear drew has just died.'
There was a young lady of Corstorphine
who adopted a psittacine orphan.
It shrieked and it cried: they threw far and wide

143

her ashes right over Corstorphine. Zoos
guard and pamper the abandoned squawkers,
tickle stories from the raunchy talkers,
shoulder a bold centenarian muse
over artists deaf as earth. 'Oho! Lear
sketched me, delirious old man, how he
shuffled about, his tabby on the sill,
a stew on the stove, a brush in his ear,
and sometimes hummed, or he buzzed like a bee,
painting parrots and all bright brave things still!'

A PLACE OF MANY WATERS

Infinitely variable water,
let seals bob in your silk or loll on Mull
where the lazy fringes rustle; let hull
and screw slew you round, blind heavy daughter
feeling for shores; keep kelpies in loch lairs,
eels gliding, malts mashing, salmon springing;
let the bullers roar to the terns winging
in from a North Sea's German Ocean airs
of pressing crashing Prussian evening blue;
give linns long fall; bubble divers bravely
down to mend the cable you love to rust;
and slant at night through lamplit cities, true
as change is true, on gap-site pools, gravely
splintering the puckering of the gust.

THE POET IN THE CITY

Rain stockaded Glasgow; we paused, changed gears,
found him solitary but cheerful in
Anniesland, with the cheerfulness you'd win,
we imagined, through schiltrons of banked fears.
The spears had a most sombre glint, as if
the forced ranks had re-closed, but there he wrote
steadily, with a peg for the wet coat
he'd dry and put on soon. Gulls cut the cliff
of those houses, we watched him follow them
intently, see them beat and hear them scream

about the invisible sea they smelt
and fish-white boats they raked from stern to stem
although their freedom was in fact his dream
of freedom with all guilts all fears unfelt.

THE NORN (1)

It was high summer, and the sun was hot.
We flew up over Perthshire, following
Christo's great-granddaughter in her swing-wing
converted crop-sprayer till plastic shot
above Schiehallion from her spinneret
Scotland-shaped and Scotland-sized, descended
silent, tough, translucent, light-attended,
catching that shoal of contours in one net.
Beneath it, what amazement; anger; some
stretching in wonder at a sky to touch;
chaos at airports, stunned larks, no more rain!
It would not burn, it would not cut. The hum
of civic protest probed like Dali's crutch.
Children ran wild under that counterpane.

THE NORN (2)

But was it art? We asked the French, who said
La nature est un temple où les vivants
sont les piliers, which was at least not wrong
but did it answer us? Old Christo's head
rolled from its box, wrapped in rough manila.
'The pillars of the temple are the dead,'
it said, 'packed up and bonded into lead.'
Jowls of hemp smelt sweet like crushed vanilla.
But his descendant in her flying-suit
carefully put the head back in its place.
'Of course it's art,' she said, 'we just use men.
Pygmalion got it inside out, poor brute.
For all they've been made art, they've not lost face.
They'll lift the polythene, be men again.'

145

THE TARGET

Then they were running with fire in their hair,
men and women were running everywhere,
women and children burning everywhere,
ovens of death were falling from the air.
Lucky seemed those at the heart of the blast
who left no flesh or ash or blood or bone,
only a shadow on dead Glasgow's stone,
when the black angel had gestured and passed.
Rhu was a demons' pit, Faslane a grave;
the shattered basking sharks that thrashed Loch Fyne
were their killer's tocsin: 'Where I am, watch;
when I raise one arm to destroy, I save
none; increase, multiply; vengeance is mine;
in no universe will man find his match.'

AFTER FALLOUT

A giant gannet buzzed our glinty probe.
Its forty-metre wing-span hid the sun.
Life was stirring, the fallout time was done.
From *a stick-nest in Ygdrasil* the globe
was hatching genes like rajahs' koh-i-noors.
Over St Kilda, house-high poppy-beds
made forests; towering sea-pinks turned the heads
of even master mariners with lures
that changed the white sea-graves to scent-drenched groves.
Fortunate Isles! The gannet bucked our ship
with a quick sidelong swoop, clapped its wings tight,
dived, and exploding through the herring droves
dragged up a flailing manta by the lip
and flew it, twisting slowly, out of sight.

THE AGE OF HERACLEUM

The jungle of Gleneagles was a long
shadow on our right as we travelled down.
Boars rummaged through the ballroom's toppled crown
of chandeliers and mashed the juicy throng

146

of giant hogweed stalks. Wild tramps with sticks
glared, kept a rough life. South in Fife we saw
the rusty buckled bridges, the firth raw
with filth and flower-heads, dead fish, dark slicks.
We stood in what had once been Princes Street.
Hogweed roots thrust, throbbed underneath for miles.
The rubble of the shops became the food
of new cracks running mazes round our feet,
and west winds blew, past shattered bricks and tiles,
millions of seeds through ruined Holyrood.

COMPUTER ERROR: NEUTRON STRIKE

No one was left to hear the long All Clear.
Hot wind swept through the streets of Aberdeen
and stirred the corpse-clogged harbour. Each machine,
each building, tank, car, college, crane, stood sheer
and clean but that a shred of skin, a hand,
a blackened child driven like tumbleweed
would give the lack of ruins leave to feed
on horrors we were slow to understand
but did. Boiling fish-floating seas slopped round
the unmanned rigs that flared into the night;
the videos ran on, sham death, sham love;
the air-conditioners kept steady sound.
An automatic foghorn, and its light
warned out to none below, and none above.

INWARD BOUND

Flapping, fluttering, like imploding porridge
being slowly uncooked on anti-gas,
the Grampians were a puny shrinking mass
of cairns and ski-tows sucked back to their orig-
ins. Pylons rumbled downwards; lighthouses
hissed into bays; reactors popped, ate earth.
We watched a fissure struggling with the girth
of old Glamis, but down it went. Boots, blouses,
hats, hands above heads, like feet-first divers
all those inhabitants pressed in to meet

badgers and stalactites, and to build in reverse
tenements deepest for late arrivers,
and domes to swim in, not to echo feet
or glow down, dim, on the draped, chanted hearse.

THE DESERT

There was a time when everything was sand.
It drifted down from Findhorn, south south south
and sifted into eye and ear and mouth
on battlefield or bed or plough-bent land.
Loose wars grew sluggish, and the bugles choked.
We saw some live in caves, and even tombs.
Mirages rose from dry Strathspey in plumes.
Scorpions appeared. Heaven's fires were stoked.
But soon they banded to bind dunes in grass,
made cactus farms, ate lizards, sank their wells.
They had their rough strong songs, rougher belief.
Did time preserve them through that narrow pass?
Or are they Guanches under conquerors' spells,
chiselled on sorry plinths in Tenerife?

THE COIN

We brushed the dirt off, held it to the light.
The obverse showed us *Scotland*, and the head
of a red deer; the antler-glint had fled
but the fine cut could still be felt. All right:
we turned it over, read easily *One Pound*,
but then the shock of Latin, like a gloss,
Respublica Scotorum, sent across
such ages as we guessed but never found
at the worn edge where once the date had been
and where as many fingers had gripped hard
as hopes their silent race had lost or gained.
The marshy scurf crept up to our machine,
sucked at our boots. Yet nothing seemed ill-starred.
And least of all the realm the coin contained.

THE SOLWAY CANAL

Slowly through the Cheviot Hills at dawn
we sailed. The high steel bridge at Carter Bar
passed over us in fog with not a car
in its broad lanes. Our hydrofoil slid on,
vibrating quietly through wet rock walls
and scarves of dim half-sparkling April mist;
a wizard with a falcon on his wrist
was stencilled on our bow. Rough waterfalls
flashed on that northern island of the Scots
as the sun steadily came up and cast
red light along the uplands and the waves,
and gulls with open beaks tore out our thoughts
through the thick glass to where the Eildons massed,
or down to the Canal's drowned borderers' graves.

A SCOTTISH JAPANESE PRINT

Lighter and lighter, not eternity,
only a morning breaking on dark fields.
The sleepers might almost throw back those shields,
jump to stations as if golden pity
could probe the grave, the beauty was so great
in that silent slowly brightening place.
No, it is the living who wait for grace,
the hare, the fox, the farmer at the gate.
And Glasgow's windows took the strong spring sun
in the corner of a water-meadow,
its towers shadowed by a pigeon's flight.
Not daisy-high, children began to run
like tumbling jewels, as in old Yeddo,
and with round eyes unwound their wild red kite.

OUTWARD BOUND

– That was the time Scotland began to move.
– Scotland move? No, it is impossible!
– It became an island, and was able
to float in the Atlantic lake and prove

crannogs no fable. Like a sea-washed log
it loved to tempt earnest geographers,
duck down and dub them drunk hydrographers,
shake itself dry, no longer log but dog.
– Was it powered? On stilts? – Amazing grace
was found in granite, it moved on pure sound.
Greenland twisted round to hear it, Key West
whistled, waved, Lanzarote's ashy face
cracked open with laughter. There was no ground
of being, only being, sweetest and best.

ON JUPITER

Scotland was found on Jupiter. That's true.
We lost all track of time, but there it was.
No one told us its origins, its cause.
A simulacrum, a dissolving view?
It seemed as solid as a terrier
shaking itself dry from a brisk black swim
in the reservoir of Jupiter's grim
crimson trustless eye. No soul-ferrier
guarded the swampy waves. Any gods there,
if they had made the thing in play, were gone,
and if the land had launched its own life out
among the echoes of inhuman air,
its launchers were asleep, or had withdrawn,
throwing their stick into a sea of doubt.

CLYDEGRAD

It was so fine we lingered there for hours.
The long broad streets shone strongly after rain.
Sunset blinded the tremble of the crane
we watched from, dazed the heliport-towers.
The mile-high buildings flashed, flushed, greyed, went dark,
greyed, flushed, flashed, chameleons under flak
of cloud and sun. The last far thunder-sack
ripped and spilled its grumble. Ziggurat-stark,
a power-house reflected in the lead
of the old twilight river leapt alive

150

lit up at every window, and a boat
of students rowed past, slid from black to red
into the blaze. But where will they arrive
with all, boat, city, earth, like them, afloat?

A GOLDEN AGE

That must have been a time of happiness.
The air was mild, the Campsie Fells had vines.
Dirigible parties left soft sky-signs
and bursts of fading music. Who could guess
what they might not accomplish, they had seas
in cities, cities in the sea; their domes
and crowded belvederes hung free, their homes
eagle-high or down among whitewashed quays.
And women sauntered often with linked arms
through night streets, or alone, or danced a maze
with friends. Perhaps it did not last. What lasts?
The bougainvillea millenniums
may come and go, but then in thistle days
a strengthened seed outlives the hardest blasts.

THE SUMMONS

The year was ending, and the land lay still.
Despite our countdown, we were loath to go,
kept padding along the ridge, the broad glow
of the city beneath us, and the hill
swirling with a little mist. Stars were right,
plans, power; only now this unforeseen
reluctance, like a slate we could not clean
of characters, yet could not read, or write
our answers on, or smash, or take with us.
Not a hedgehog stirred. We sighed, climbed in, locked.
If it was love we felt, would it not keep,
and travel where we travelled? Without fuss
we lifted off, but as we checked and talked
a far horn grew to break that people's sleep.

151

From the Video Box

If you ask what my favourite programme is
it has to be that strange world jigsaw final.
After the winner had defeated all his rivals
with harder and harder jigsaws, he had to prove his mettle
by completing one last absolute mindcrusher
on his own, under the cameras, in less than a week.
We saw, but he did not, what the picture would be:
the mid-Atlantic, photographed from a plane,
as featureless a stretch as could be found,
no weeds, no flotsam, no birds, no oil, no ships,
the surface neither stormy nor calm, but ordinary,
a light wind on a slowly rolling swell.
Hand-cut by a fiendish jigger to simulate,
but not to have, identical beaks and bays,
it seemed impossible; but the candidate –
he said he was a stateless person, called himself Smith –
was impressive: small, dark, nimble, self-contained.
The thousands of little grey tortoises were scattered
on the floor of the studio; we saw the clock; he started.
His food was brought to him, but he hardly ate.
He had a bed, with the light only dimmed to a weird blue,
never out. By the first day he had established
the edges, saw the picture was three metres long
and appeared to represent (dear God!) the sea.
Well, it was a man's life, and the silence
(broken only by sighs, click of wood, plop of coffee
in paper cups) that kept me fascinated.
Even when one hand was picking the edge-pieces
I noticed his other hand was massing sets
of distinguishing ripples or darker cross-hatching or
incipient wave-crests; his mind,
if not his face, worked like a sea.
It was when he suddenly rose from his bed
at two, on the third night, went straight over
to one piece and slotted it into a growing central patch,
then back to bed, that I knew he would make it.
On the sixth day he looked haggard and slow,
with perhaps a hundred pieces left,
of the most dreary unmarked lifeless grey.

The camera showed the clock more frequently.
He roused himself, and in a quickening burst
of activity, with many false starts, began
to press that inhuman insolent remnant together.
He did it, on the evening of the sixth day.
People streamed onto the set. Bands played.
That was fine. But what I liked best
was the last shot of the completed sea,
filling the screen; then the saw-lines disappeared,
till almost imperceptibly the surface moved
and it was again the real Atlantic, glad
to distraction to be released, raised
above itself in growing gusts, allowed
to roar as rain drove down and darkened,
allowed to blot, for a moment, the orderer's hand.

26

What was the best programme?
Oh, it was Giotto's O.
I don't argue the case
that it really was the past,
tapped under conditions
made suddenly favourable.
But how could any actor
so unpreparedly, so
swiftly yet so surely and
so gloriously seize
a sheet of pure white paper
and with a black loaded brush
paint a perfect circle?
The camera was so close
that no trick or device
could have stayed undetected.
No, it was Giotto's O.
The papal envoy, I observed,
crossed himself at the sight –
needlessly, there was no magic
either black or white, it
was only the life of a man
concentrated down

to his finger-tips in the great
final ease of creation
which in its silence and
no longer laboriously
circles round and out.

27

The programme that stays most in my mind
was one you called the Dance of the Letters.
The graphics here was altogether
crisp and bright and strong and real.
First that gallows, with the dust
whirling across the square to sting
a blackened and unfeeling face
and tear at the unreadable placard
pinned to its slowly twisting chest
resolved itself into a T.
Then the car, in bird's-eye view,
crawling through narrow streets to bang
its bomb-load and its girl martyr
into a crowded market-place
stopped, became a fiery H.
Mothers, children, grandfathers, all
knew how to line the desert dirt-road
in a few black rags, and stretch out bowls
in their twig arms or hold out only
arms, till their appeal froze
in stifling fly-black heat to form
an E. But then another E
was gently, tentatively drawn
from the hard, half-shining prongs
of a rake; the gnarled gardener
was keeping his patch clean and rich,
weedless and airy, able to deliver
the vegetables of the year.
In a courtyard, shaded with awnings,
where a tethered, slew-mouthed camel chewed,
one red earthen water-jar
as old as history waited in its stand,
turning at last into an N.

A fisherwoman, pregnant, walked
slowly along a rocky shore,
but then transformed into a ship
with blowing spinnaker sailed out
in her whole woman's life to break
silence only with the whipping
of the sheets and with the song
she or the wind threw back to us.
She left us, melted into the white
of a D that rang out through the blue.

The Dowser

With my forked branch of Lebanese cedar
I quarter the dunes like downs and guide
an invisible plough far over the sand.
But how to quarter such shifting acres
when the wind melts their shapes, and shadows
mass where all was bright before,
and landmarks walk like wraiths at noon?
All I know is that underneath,
how many miles no one can say,
an unbroken water-table waits
like a lake; it has seen no bird or sail
in its long darkness, and no man;
not even pharaohs dug so far
for all their thirst, or thirst of glory,
or thrust-power of ten thousand slaves.
I tell you I can smell it though,
that water. I am old and black
and I know the manners of the sun
which makes me bend, not break. I lose
my ghostly footprints without complaint.
I put every mirage in its place.
I watch the lizard make its lace.
Like one not quite blind I go
feeling for the sunken face.
So hot the days, the nights so cold,
I gather my white rags and sigh
but sighing step so steadily
that any vibrance in so deep
a lake would never fail to rise
towards the snowy cedar's bait.
Great desert, let your sweetness wake.

'Dear man, my love goes out in waves'

Dear man, my love goes out in waves
and breaks. Whatever is, craves.
Terrible the cage
to see all life from, brilliantly about,
crowds, pavements, cars, or hear the common shout
of goals in a near park.
But now the black bars arc
blue in my breath – split – part –
I'm out – it's art,
it's love, it's rage –

Standing in rage in decent air
will never clear the place of care.
Simply to be
should be enough, in the same city, and let
absurd despair tramp and roar off-set.
Be satisfied with it,
the gravel and the grit
the struggling eye can't lift,
the veils that drift,
the weird to dree.

Press close to me at midnight as
you say goodbye; that's what it has
to offer, life
I mean. Into the frost with you; into
the bed with me; and get the light out too.
Better to shake unseen
and let real darkness screen
the shadows of the heart,
the vacant part-
ner, husband, wife.

Rules for Dwarf-Throwing

1. If a dwarf is thrown through a glass window or glass door, he must wear gloves and a suitable mask.

2. If a dwarf is thrown through a burning hoop, extinguishers must be provided.

3. If a dwarf is thrown down a well, the organizers must ensure that the bottom of the well is dry, and is covered by leaves to a depth of three inches.

4. If a dwarf is to be thrown across the path of an oncoming train, the thrower must previously satisfy the organizers that he bears no personal malice to the throwee.

5. If a dwarf is thrown into a pond or river, he must wear a wetsuit and need not be tightly bound.

6. If dwarfs are thrown at night, they may be painted with phosphorescent paint, so that the point of impact may be clearly established.

7. If a dwarf refuses to be bound in the usual way before throwing, he may be put in a straitjacket of the requisite size.

8. If a dwarf utters any sound whatsoever, either in flight or at the moment of impact, the throw will be disqualified.

9. If a jockey impersonates a dwarf, and wins a competition because his light weight allows him to be thrown farthest, he will be liable to a fine of £1000 or three years imprisonment.

10. It is strictly forbidden, in dwarf-throwing literature and publicity, to refer to dwarfs as 'persons of restricted growth' or 'small people'.

Stein on Venus

A crater on Venus is to be named
after Gertrude Stein.
(News item, 1991)

Where I stand, there I reign.
What is not subject is objectless.
Who knows how far my train of skirts
skirts other craters, on their knees
without evening or morning? When it is
there could ever be an end to power
I do not need to stride to tell you
or straddle a rock with a slap or scoop
fistfuls of dust to stiffen the sift –
it is all time down the red drain
to me, planted here in full pluck,
my grizzle bald as a dollar, set,
I said set, and who is going to move me?
– Only the great god Venus who
dibbled me into the rubble, saying
Water yourself! He laughed and left,
but trails his grim throne still, I know,
without servants, through sulphur, over slag,
endlessly I would say. Who loves him?
Some are standing stones, like me.
Some lie flat as dolmens. All
wait for nothing but the hiss of storms,
the crimson seething, the particle clatter,
the lightning-shattered smog of ochre,
the settling down and the rising up,
the impregnated immobilities!
God of the sun and ash, I take you
as you take me, I breathe, I sweat,
I dash my invisible waves as every
stone does, squeezing its roused seas
up and out as if they could find
beaches of meanest marram long dreamed.

Eros

Of course I want you up here, you can make it.
It's been so long and I'm so cold. The wind
sweeps across the Circus with rain in it,
lashes me till I'm streaming, what protection
do you think this wisp of drape is? Worse,
I'm tarnishing from the sharp traffic fumes
when all I want to do is shine and shine,
point my bow off and out and hit it –
what? – anything and anyone that loves
a flash of gleaming chest and a wingspread
as natural and as supernatural
as if I'd dropped among you at that instant
and not a hundred years ago, in my
not quite eternal youth. I'm helmeted
with messages that pulse far over London.
What I transmit I receive, the love you send me,
of course you do, all of you, I feel it
throbbing and crackling through my aluminium.
I am six feet tall. I want to be embraced.
I long for you to climb up here beside me,
twine your legs about me, clasp my neck,
press close to my good looks and kiss me so
that everyone can see, that none can doubt it.
Watch the fountain. You are almost there. See
I am totally ready for my lover.
He will jump on me, warm, thighs, arms,
lastly lips – and that will be my happiness,
in the midst and thunder of the city.

Macaronicon
For Tom Scott at 75

That night I saw a moor with scattered fires.
Grey smoke drifted through to break the gleam
of weapons abandoned. Figures, call them no more,
skulked in and out of the smoke-swirls, half-crouched,
knifed any bundles that still stirred or groaned,

cut rings off to test any playing possum.
No moon, only the fires. Ane barand steid,
the flichter an the smeek, the wappins grundit,
the besy fowk like sheddas getherin there
tae pyke oot ony gliff o life, kickin
corp an hauf-corp for a tellin grane,
howkin the gowd rings, leavin the braw een
for corbies. Nuit d'un champ de misères,
petits feux partout, et la fumée qui roule
parmi les armes, les mourants et les morts,
les furtives figures qui frôlent et tuent
ces blessés, arrachant pendant le râle
doigt, anneau, joyau, vie et tout.
Et la lune s'endormit. Mi ritrovai
per uno campo oscuro che la guerra
aveva guastato, corpo sul corpo, gemito
sul gemito, fuoco sul fuoco, fumo
sul fumo, ed i furfatori infernali
robbing and hacking until the very dead
yowlit an chirmit Oh que c'est lointain
et fort, l'espoir des hommes, benigna pax!

Difference   .

The endless variousness is all for praises.
The faces, passing, never make an empire.
And Iskander stopped writing in Abkhazian,
Aigi in Chuvash, Rytkheu in Chukcha.
So much the worse, so much the worse. You think not?
You'd rather have the second-best as long as
millions get it? – Mission, you cry, the mission!
we want the mass to move en bloc, not crunch on
caltrops, inessentials, unideals!
We catch an awkward squad we do a brainwash
with promises of universal favour
far beyond the sheep-fanks, fish-holes, shamans.
Why not – it's easy – cut fish-holes in Russian?
– The endless variousness evolves, the empire
expires in frozen edicts, you can skate there

but soon you're off the edge, and then there's no one
bar the unassimilated – *bar-bar, bar-bar* –
to save you, and why should they, since you doomed them
to hold their tongue, and everything that made them
to their hearts, flags burning a locked drawer,
songs that are not alien to the alien,
accreted stinging stories mocking labials
where you are a *bar-bar* to them. The faces
pass, the individuals, how there can be such
difference we do not know but what we do know
is that an absolute instinct loves it different,
the world, the dialectic, the packed coaches
whistling at daybreak through the patched countries.

Persuasion

You never thought much of the darkness, did you?
You wanted everything so open, open –
I said it could not be – you laughed, and shook me,
and pointed me and swivelled me to windows,
doors, rivers, skies – said it must be, must issue
right out if it was to have any honour –
what: love? – yes: love; it must seal up its burrow,
must take a stair or two, a flight or two, for
poles, horizons, convoys, elevations –
but tender still to backcourts and dim woodlands.
Oh, never ask where darkness is if light can
break down the very splinters of the jambs – be
sure I know you can take in the sunlight
through every pore and nothing will be blinded
or shrivelled up like moth in flame or crippled
by some excess of nakedness – just give it,
your intelligence, your faith I really mean, your
faith, that's it, to see the streets so brilliant
after gales you really can go out there,
you really can have something of that gladness,
many things under the sun, and not disheartened,
so many in their ways going beside you.

An Abandoned Culvert

The daffodils sang shrill within the culvert.
Their almost acid notes amazed the darkness
culverts are happiest with. They could not cower,
the yellow birds, pure cries on stilts, conundrums
to burst the reason of those mineral courses.
Five stubborn half-fluted half-ragged non-fluting trumpets
blared the dank brickfall grit into submission.
Whatever daffodils can say, they said it
louder and sharper than the stalagmites they
might have been, if all the timorous ages
had managed to conspire against some thrusting
of the dumb seed that could not know, yet knew, it
had to unapologetically
proclaim a yellow and not golden treasure
unyielding to the kisses of the digger.

A City

– What was all that then? – What? – *That*. – That was *Glasgow*.
It's a film, an epic, lasts for, anyway
keep watching, it's not real, so everything is
melting at the edges and could go, you have to
remember some of it was shot in Moscow,
parts in Chicago, and then of course the people
break up occasionally, they're only graphics,
look there's two businessmen gone zigzag, they'll be
off-screen in one moment, yes, I thought so.
– What a sky though. – Ah well, the sky is listed,
change as it may. It's a peculiar platinum
with roary sunset flecks and fissures, rigging
was best against it, gone now, don't regret it,
move on, and if you wait you'll see some children,
oh it's a fine effect, maybe they're real, some
giant children pulling down a curtain
of platinum and scarlet stuff as airy
as it seems strong, and they'll being to play there,

163

bouncing their shrill cries till it's too dark to
catch a shadow running along the backcloth,
and they still won't go home, despite the credits.
– You mean the film goes on, beyond the credits?
– You'll have to wait and see, won't you? It's worth it.
– I'm not persuaded even of its existence.
– What, *Glasgow*? – The city, not the film. – The city
is the film. – Oh come on. – I tell you. – Right then,
look. Renfield Street, marchers, banners, slogans.
Read the message, hear the chant. – Lights! Camera!
– But where are the children? – That I grant you;
somewhere, huge presences; shouting, laughter;
hunch-cuddy-hunch against a phantom housewall.

Il Traviato

That's my eyes at their brightest and biggest.
It's belladonna. I've a friend who. Not that
I'd ever use too much, did once, came out of
delirium after a week of sweats, you learn. But
I'm so pale now, some men like the contrast
as I stand in the park with my eyes burning,
or glide among the poplars, they're thin as I am
but seem to manage, get their light, get nourished
as I get trade although the Wraith's my nickname.
I ought to be in bed, probably, maybe.
In any case my lover sends me out now,
he says it's all I'm good for, bring some money.
He hides my razor till I'm 'interesting',
a chalky portrait ruffed in my black stubble.
I mustn't be too hard on him. The years we.
It all comes down to what kind of constant
you believe in, doesn't it, not mathematics
but as if you had the faintest brilliance
that was only yours, not to let any sickness
douse it, or despair creeping with a snuffer.
I sometimes think I wish it could be ended
– those hard-faced brutes that hit you at the climax –

but then I go on, don't I, as everyone
should, pressing through the streets with glances
for all and everything, not to miss crumbs of
life, drops of the crowded flowing wonder.

Aunt Myra (1901-1989)

A horse in a field in a picture is easy.
A man in a room with a fan, we wonder.
It might be whirring blades in steamy downtown –
but no, it's what she's left beside her dance-cards.
How she sat out a foxtrot at the Plaza
and fanned her brow, those far-off flirty Twenties
he opens and shuts with an unpractised gesture
that leaves the years half-laughing at the pathos
of the clumsy, until rising strings have swept them
dancing again into silence. The room darkens
with a blue lingering glow above the roof-tops
but the man still stands there, holding up the dangling
dance-cards by their tiny attached pencils.
The cords which are so light seem to him heavy
as if they were about to take the strain of
tender evenings descending into memory.
Something is hard, not easy, though it's clearly
a man, a fan, a woman, a room, a picture.

Urban Gunfire

'Civilians' are not really, truly, people.
As regimes fall, they're only 'caught in crossfire'.
Expendablest of the expendable, they
crawl, or if they're lucky someone drags them,
to doorways where they slump and shake till nightfall.
How great it must be not to be civilian

or anything but gun in hand, young, mobile,
slogan-fuelled better than machines are,
you cannot even hear the shattered housewife,
far less see her blood and bags and bread, it's
bullet time between you and your sniper,
hot streaks go shopping, nothing else goes shopping,
no one is out there in the open, we are,
we are it and it is where they vanish
like a clapped piece of tawdry human magic,
too feeble to be seen by psyched-up fighters.
Their cries are in another world. The trigger
is steady as they roll about the tarmac.
And it goes on as if it could not finish.

Fires

What is that place, my father and my mother,
you have gone to, I think of, in the ashes
of the air and not the earth, better to go there
than under stones or in any remembrance
but mine and that of others who once loved you,
fewer year on year. It is midsummer
and till my voice broke, *Summer suns are glowing*
I loved to sing and *One fine day* to hear from
some thin wild old gramophone that carried
its passion across the Rutherglen street, invisibly
played again and again – I thought of that person,
him or her, as taking me to a country
far high sunny where I knew to be happy
was only a moment, a puttering flame in the fireplace
but burning all the misery to cinders
if it could, a sift of dross like what we mourn for
as caskets sink with horrifying blandness
into a roar, into smoke, into light, into almost nothing.
The not quite nothing I praise it and I write it.

A Pedlar

An old man selling joy comes round here sometimes.
His case weighs down, no one seems to want it.
Buttonless coat and battered cardboard stand there
like diffidence made monumental. Promise –
of anything – never seemed further, blanker.
Who would not slam a door on such a scarecrow?
If any lingered, his entire persuasion
was to look at them, hangdog, hand on case-lock,
waiting to be asked to unroll treasures.
Not that way, never that way, hopeless person!
Even his trudging back was not reproachful.
– But anyway there came a day, today, be honest,
when if something changeable bluff bright cloudy
in the air and such a brash sun shouldering branches
recharged his speech I can only imagine –
but he flung open the case and suddenly was saying
'What is not there is hardly worth desiring,
do you not agree? Is it not fine? Others
have said so, whenever I could elicit
a bit of truth from pursed lips. Pursed and zipped is
what I mean! You tell them it's quite costly
they vanish behind their mortises. Pedlars?
No thanks. Yet four wheels to the hypermarket –
get boys to load your boot with wine and salmon –
a shark steak for a laugh, some avocados –
perhaps a large pavlova if *they're* coming –
will not purr back with it, don't be deluded,
since only what you do not want to pay for
is what I have: I do not sell for money.
But if you can lay out a little pain, it's business.
Break a pig of disappointments, frustrations.
An old billfold of hopes deferred? Only
if it aches, aches. Look at what I have here,
this, and these. The price is not beyond you?'
'No no,' I said, 'no, it's not, no, I'll have some.'

Planet Wave

*This sequence of poems, commissioned by the Cheltenham
International Jazz Festival, and set to music by
Tommy Smith, was first performed in the Cheltenham
Town Hall on 4 April 1997.*

IN THE BEGINNING
(20 Billion B.C.)

Don't ask me and don't tell me. I was there.
It was a bang and it was big. I don't know
what went before, I came out with it.
Think about that if you want my credentials.
Think about that, me, it, imagine it
as I recall it now, swinging in my spacetime hammock,
nibbling a moon or two, watching you.
What am I? You don't know. It doesn't matter.
I am the witness, I am not in the dock.
I love matter and I love anti-matter.
Listen to me, listen to my patter.

Oh what a day (if it was day) that was!
It was as if a fist had been holding fast
one dense packed particle too hot to keep
and the fingers had suddenly sprung open
and the burning coal, the radiant mechanism
had burst and scattered the seeds of everything,
out through what was now space, out
into the pulse of time, out, my masters,
out, my friends, so, like a darting shoal,
like a lion's roar, like greyhounds released,
like blown dandelions, like Pandora's box,
like a shaken cornucopia, like an ejaculation –

I was amazed at the beauty of it all,
those slowly cooling rosy clouds of gas,
wave upon wave of hydrogen and helium,
spirals and rings and knots of fire, silhouettes
of dust in towers, thunderheads, tornadoes;
and then the stars, and the blue glow of starlight
lapislazuliing the dust-grains –

I laughed, rolled like a ball, flew like a dragon,
zigzagged and dodged the clatter of meteorites
as they clumped and clashed and clustered into
worlds, into this best clutch of nine
whirled in the Corrievreckan of the Sun.
The universe had only just begun.
I'm off, my dears. My story's still to run!

THE EARLY EARTH
(3 Billion B.C.)

Planets, planets – they seem to have settled
into their orbits, round their golden lord,
their father, except he's not their father,
they were all born together, in that majestic wave
of million-degree froth and jet and muck:
who would have prophesied the dancelike separation,
the nine globes, with their moons and rings, rare –
do you know how rare it is, dear listeners,
dear friends, do you know how rare you are?
Don't you want to be thankful? You suffer too much?
I'll give you suffering, but first comes thanks.

Think of that early wild rough world of earth:
lurid, restless, cracking, groaning, heaving,
swishing through space garbage and flak,
cratered with a thousand dry splashdowns
painted over in molten granite. Think of hell,
a mineral hell of fire and smoke. You're there.
What's it all for? Is this the lucky planet?
Can you down a pint of lava, make love
to the Grand Canyon, tuck a thunderbolt
in its cradle? Yes and no, folks, yes and no.
You must have patience with the story.

I took myself to the crest of a ridge
once it was pushed up and cooled.
There were more cloudscapes than earthquakes.
You could walk on rock and feel rain.
You shivered but smiled in the fine tang.

169

Then I came down to stand in the shallows
of a great ocean, my collar up to the wind,
but listen, it was more than the wind I heard,
it was life at last, emerging from the sea,
shuffling, sliding, sucking, scuttling, so small
that on hands and knees I had to strain my eyes.
A trail of half-transparent twitchings!
A scum of algae! A greening! A breathing!
And no one would stop them, volcanoes wouldn't stop them!
How far would they go? What would they not try?
I punched the sky, my friends, I punched the sky.

END OF THE DINOSAURS
(65 Million B.C.)

If you want life, this is something like it.
I made myself a tree-house, and from there
I could see distant scrubby savannas
but mostly it was jungle, lush to bursting
with ferns, palms, creepers, reeds, and the first flowers.
Somewhere a half-seen slither of giant snakes,
a steamy swamp, a crocodile-drift
in and out of sunlight. But all this, I must tell you,
was only background for the rulers of life,
the dinosaurs. Who could stand against them?
They pounded the earth, they lazed in lakes,
they razored through the sultry air.

                              Hear,
if you will, the scrunchings of frond and branch
but also of joint and gristle. It's not a game.
I watched a tyrannosaurus rise on its hindlegs
to slice a browsing diplodocus, just like that,
a hiss, a squirm, a shake, a supper –
velociraptors scattered like rabbits.

It didn't last. It couldn't? I don't know.
Were they too big, too monstrous, yet wonderful
with all the wonder of terror. Were there other plans?
I saw the very day the asteroid struck:

170

mass panic, mass destruction, mass smoke and mass ash
that broke like a black wave over land and sea,
billowing, thickening, choking, until no sun
could pierce the pall and no plants grew and no
lizards however terrible found food and no
thundering of armoured living tons disturbed
the forest floor and there was no dawn roar,
only the moans, only the dying groans
of those bewildered clinker-throated ex-time-lords,
only, at the end, skulls and ribs and hatchless
eggs in swamps and deserts
left for the inheritors –
my friends, that's you and me
branched on a different tree:
what shall we do, or be?

IN THE CAVE
(30,000 B.C.)

Dark was the cave where I discovered man,
but he made it, in his own way, bright.
The cavern itself was like a vast hall
within a labyrinth of tunnels. Children
set lamps on ledges. Women fanned a hearth.
Suddenly with a jagged flare of torches
men trooped in from the hunt, threw down
jagged masses of meat, peeled off furs
by the fire till they were half-naked, glistening
with sweat, stocky intelligent ruffians,
brought the cave alive with rapid jagged speech.
You expected a grunt or two? Not so.
And music, surely not? You never heard
such music, I assure you, as the logs crackled
and the meat sizzled, when some with horns and drums
placed echoes in the honeycomb of corridors.
This was no roaring of dinosaurs.

I joined them for their meal. They had a bard,
a storyteller. Just like me, I said.
I told him about distant times. He interrupted.

171

'I don't think I believe that. Are you a shaman?
If so, where's your reindeer coat? Have another drink.
If you're a shape-shifter, I'm a truth-teller.
Drink up, we call it beer, it's strong, it's good.
You should've been out with us today,
it isn't every day you catch a mammoth,
keep us fed for a week, fur too, tusks –
nothing wasted. Spears and arrows both,
that's what you need, plus a good crowd a boys,
goo' crowda boys. Take s'more beer, go on.
See mamm'ths? Mamm'ths're fuck'n stupit.
Once they're down they can't get up. Fuck em.
Y'know this, y'know this, ole shaman-man,
we'll be here long after mamm'ths're gone.'

He stumbled to his feet, seized a huge torch and ran
along the wall, making such a wave of sparks
the painted mammoths kicked and keeled once more.

A deep horn gave that movie flicker its score.

THE GREAT FLOOD
(10,000 B.C.)

Rain, rain, and rain again, and still more rain,
rain and lightning, rain and mist, a month of downpours,
till the earth quaked gruffly somewhere and sent
tidal waves over the Middle Sea,
tidal waves over the Middle East,
tidal wave and rain and tidal wave
to rave and rove over road and river and grove.
I skimmed the water-level as it rose:
invisible the delta! gone the headman's hut!
drowned at last even the stony jebel!

I groaned at whole families swept out to sea.
Strong horses swam and swam but sank at last.
Little treasures, toys, amulets were licked
off pitiful ramshackle village walls.
Weapons, with the hands that held them, vanished.

172

So what to do? Oh never underestimate
those feeble scrabbling panting gill-less beings!
Hammers night and day on the high plateau!
Bitumen smoking! Foremen swearing! A boat,
an enormous boat, a ship, a seafarer,
caulked, battened, be-sailed, oar-banked, crammed
with life, human, animal, comestible,
holy with hope, bobbing above the tree-tops,
set off to shouts and songs into the unknown
through rags and carcases and cold storks' nests.

The waters did go down. A whaleback mountain
shouldered up in a brief gleam of sludge,
nudged the ark and grounded it. Hatches gaped.
Heads smelt the air. Some bird was chirping.
And then a rainbow: I laughed, it was too much.
But as they tottered out with their bundles,
their baskets of tools, their goats, their babies,
and broke like a wave over the boulders and mosses,
I thought it was a better wave than the wet one
that had almost buried them all.

                                        Water
we came from, to water we may return.
But keep webbed feet at arm's length! Build!
That's what I told them: re-build, but build!

THE GREAT PYRAMID
(2,500 B.C.)

A building of two million blocks of stone
brought from beyond the Nile by barge and sledge,
dragged up on ramps, trimmed and faced smooth
with bronze chisels and sandstone pads, what a gleam,
what a dazzle of a tomb, what mathematics
in that luminous limestone point against the blue,
the blue above and the yellow below,
the black above and the silver below,
the stars like sand-grains, the pyramid joining them –

You should have seen it, my friends, I must confess
it made a statement to me, and you can scrub
conventional wisdom about the megalomania
of mummies awaiting the lift-off to eternity.
The architects, the surveyors, the purveyors,
the laundresses and cooks, and the brawny gangs
who were not slaves, they would go on strike
if some vizier was stingy with grain or beer:
it was the first mass effort to say
We're here, we did this, this is not nature
but geometry, see it from the moon some day!

Oh but the inauguration, the festivity, the holiday –
I joined the throng, dear people, how could I not?
The sun gave its old blessing, gold and hot and high.
The procession almost rose to meet it:
what was not white linen was lapis-lazuli,
what was not lapis-lazuli was gold,
there was a shining, a stiff rustling, a solemnity,
the pharaoh and his consort carried in golden chairs,
the bodyguards were like bronze statues walking,
there were real desert men with hawks, severe
as hawks themselves, there were scribes and singers,
black dancing-girls oiled to black gold – wild –
and then the long powerful snake of the workers
which rippled from the Nile to the four great faces
and coiled about them for the dedication.

And the bursting wave of music, the brilliant discords,
the blare, the triumph, the steps of the sound-lords
bore away like a storm my storyteller's words.

ON THE VOLGA
(922 A.D.)

I fancied a change, bit of chill, nip in the air,
went up into Russia, jogged along the Volga,
quite brisk, breath like steam, blood on the go,
ready for anything, you know the feeling.
But I was not as ready as I thought.

174

I came upon a camp of Vikings, traders
bound south for the Black Sea, big men, fair,
tattooed, their ships at anchor in the river.
Their chief had died, I was to witness
the ritual of cremation. It is so clear –
dear people, I must speak and you must hear –

A boat was dragged on shore, faggots were stacked,
they dressed the dead man in cloth of gold, laid him
in a tent on deck. Who would die with him?
A girl volunteered – yes, a true volunteer –
walked about singing, not downcast, stood
sometimes laughing, believe me, talking to friends.
What did she think of the dog that was cut in two,
thrown into the ship? Nothing, it was what was done.
The horses? The chief must have his beasts
by his side on that black journey. She,
when her time had come, went into six tents
one by one, and lay with the men there.
Each entered her gently, saying 'Tell your master
I did this only for love of you.' Strong drink
was given her, cup after cup. Stumbling, singing,
she was lifted onto the ship, laid down, held,
stabbed by a grim crone and strangled simultaneously
by two strong men, so no one could say who killed her.
Shields were beaten with staves to drown her cries.

Sex and death, drink and fire – the fourth was to come.
The ship was torched, caught quickly, spat, crackled,
burned, birchwood, tent-cloth, flesh, cloth of gold
melted in the blaze that was fanned even faster
by a storm blowing up from the west, sending
wave after wave of smoke in flight across the river.

My friends, do you want to know what you should feel?
I can't tell you, but feel you must. My story's real.

THE MONGOLS
(1200-1300 A.D.)

The Pope sent a letter to the Great Khan, saying
'We do not understand you. Why do you not obey?
We are under the direct command of Heaven.'
The Great Khan replied to the Pope, saying
'We do not understand you. Why do you not obey?
We are under the direct command of Heaven.'
I must admit I turned a couple of cartwheels
when I found these letters. Mongol chutzpah,
I thought, something new in the world, black comedy
you never get from the solemn Saracens.
Why not? Heaven has given them the earth
from Lithuania to Korea, they ride
like the wind over a carpet of bones.
They have laws, they record, they study the stars.
They are a wonder, but what are they for?

I stood in waves of grass, somewhere in Asia
(that's a safe address), chewing dried lamb
and scanning the low thundery sky,
when a column of Mongol soldiers came past,
halted, re-formed, were commended by their shaman
to the sky-god Tengri who was bending the blue
in order to bless them. Instruments appeared
as if from nowhere, a band, war music
but very strange, stopped as suddenly,
except for the beat of kettledrums as the troop
moved forward. Were they refreshed, inspired?
Who knows? But oh that measured conical bob
of steel caps, gleam of lacquered leather jerkins,
indefatigable silent wolf-lope!
Were they off to make rubble of some great city?
I think they were off to enlarge the known world.
They trotted out of sight; the horsemen followed;
a cold wind followed that, with arrows of rain.
Even in my felt jacket I shivered. Yet –

yet they were there to shake the mighty in their seats.
They were like nature, dragons, volcanoes. Keep awake!
Are you awake, dear people? Are you ready for the Horde,
the page-turner, the asteroid, the virtual sword?

MAGELLAN
(1521 A.D.)

Cliffs of Patagonia, coldest of coasts,
and the ships sweeping south-west into the strait
which was to be Magellan's: like St Elmo's fire
I played in the rigging, I was tingling, it was good
to see the navigator make determination
his quadrant and his compass into the unknown.
A mutiny? Always hang ringleaders. He did.
One ship wrecked, one deserted? Right. Right.
On with the other three. This channel of reefs,
a wild month needling through, cursing the fogs,
crossing himself as he saw the land of fire,
Tierra del Fuego, flaring its petroleum hell,
then out at last into what seemed endless waves –
Magellan stared at a watery third of the world.
West! West and north! What squalls! What depths!
What sea-monsters I watched from the crow's-nest!
The starving and parching below, the raving, the rats
for dinner, the gnawing of belts! Magellan held
his piercing eye and salt-white beard straight on
to landfall, to the Marianas and the Philippines and
to death. I shuddered at that beach of blood
where he was hacked to pieces. Would you not?

And would you not rejoice that his lieutenant
sailed on, sailed west, sailed limping back,
one tattered ship, sailed home again to Spain
to prove the world was round. And they would need
more ships, for it was mostly water. A ball
with no edge you could fall from – that seemed fine.
But a wet ball in space, what could hold it together?
Every triumph left a trail of questions.
Just as it should, I told the geographers.

177

Don't you agree, folks, that's the electric prod
to keep us on the move? Don't care for prods,
put your head in a bag, that's what I say.
Well, I'm given to saying things like that,
I'm free.

    Great Ferdinand Magellan,
sleep in peace beneath the seas.
The world's unlocked, and you gave us the keys.

COPERNICUS
(1543 A.D.)

In the Baltic there are many waves,
but in Prussian fields I saw, and did not see,
the wave of thought that got the earth to move.
Copernicus's Tower, as they call it,
took its three storeys to a viewing platform,
open, plenty of night, no telescope though.
I used to watch the light go on, then off,
and a dark figure occlude a star
as he would see the moon do. Moon and sun
swung round the earth, unless you were blind.
No. Earth and moon swung round the sun
and earth swung round itself. Mars, Venus,
all, a family, a system, and the system was solar.

Who was he, and does it matter? No stories
are told about this man who kicked the earth
from its false throne. Luther called him a fool
but Luther was the fool. He had servants,
rode a horse, healed the sick, heard cases,
administered a province, but his big big eyes
smouldered like worlds still unadministered.
Big hands too – but he never married.
War swirled round his enclave, peasants starved,
colleagues fled, he stayed in the smoking town –
something of iron there. A play lampooned him
but nothing could stop this patient revolutionary.
I heard them knock at the door of his death-chamber

178

to bring him the book of his life's labours
but I doubt if he saw it – he gave no sign –
that tremendous title *On the Revolutions*
(and what a pun that was) *of the Heavenly Spheres*
floated above the crumpled haemorrhage and sang
like an angel, a human angel cast loose at last
to voyage in a universe that would no more stand still
than the clouds forming and re-forming
over Copernicus's Tower.

                I looked from the roof
till it was dark and starry, and I knew my travels
were just beginning: the Magellanic Clouds
wait for those who have climbed Magellan's shrouds.